NORTH COUNTRY

SHANE WHI

ISBN-10: 1-56163-435-2
ISBN-13: 978-1-56163-435-4
© 2005 Shane White
Library of Congress Control Number: 2005927719

Printed in China

3   2   1

Comicslit is an imprint
and trademark of

NANTIER ∘ BEALL ∘ MINOUSTCHINE
Publishing inc.
new york

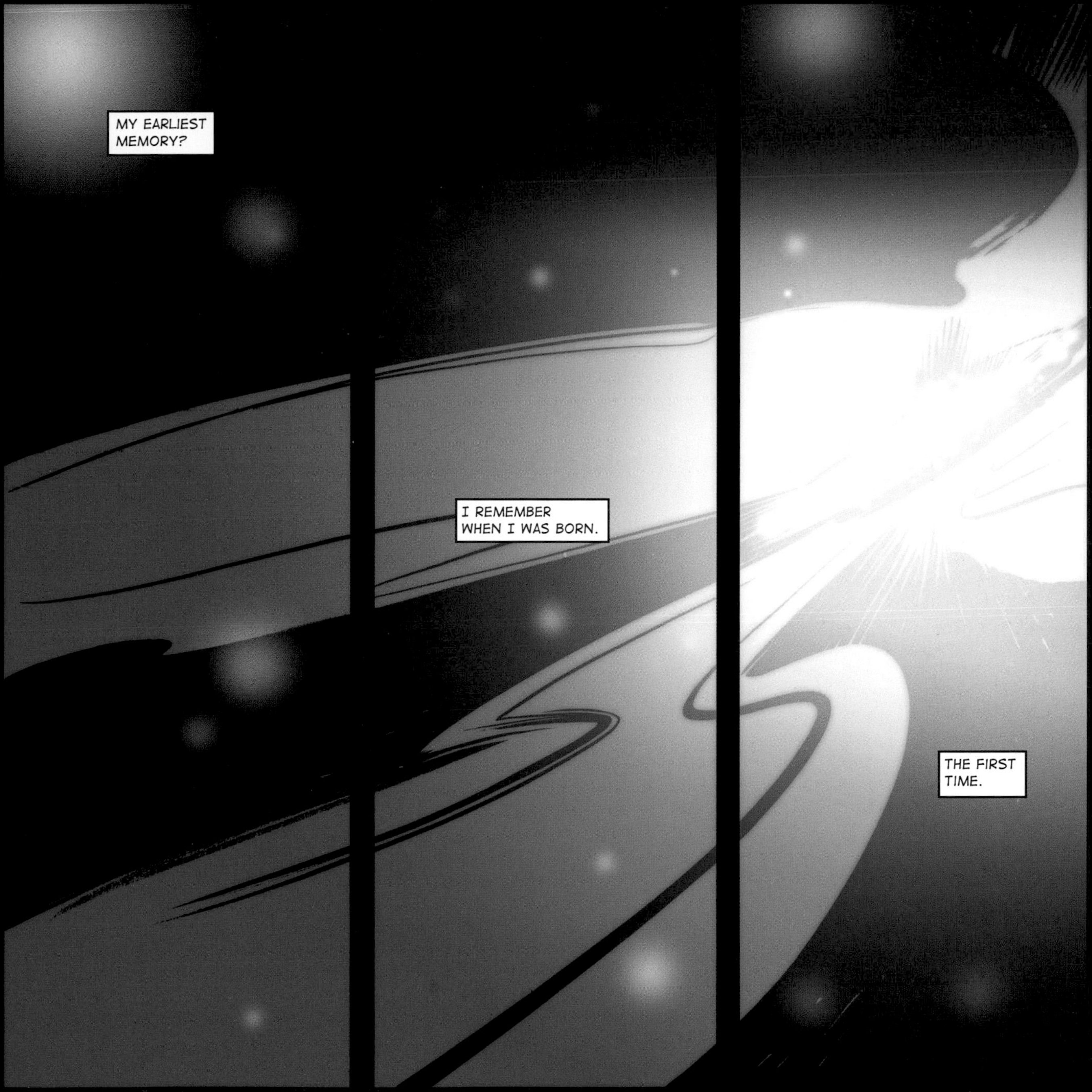
MY EARLIEST MEMORY?
I REMEMBER WHEN I WAS BORN.
THE FIRST TIME.

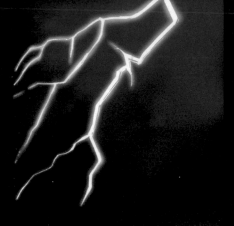

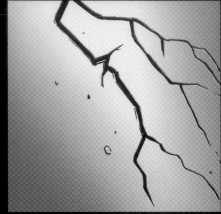

IT WAS A STRUGGLE FROM THE START.

MY DISTASTE FOR THE FOOD AND CROWDING OF FAMILY PUSHED ME AWAY.

MY DESIRE TO LEAVE WAS FAR GREATER...

...THAN THE DANGER THAT LAY BEFORE ME.

IT WOULD BE MY FIRST MISTAKE...

...AND MY LAST.

THERE WAS A DULL THROB IN MY NECK, WHITE HOT AS I GREW COLDER.

A METALLIC TASTE LINGERED IN MY THROAT AS ETERNAL SLEEP CAME ON.

I FELT MYSELF DISENGAGE FROM THE BODY, YET I STILL EXISTED.

THE INFINITE DARKNESS SUSTAINED ME AS I FLOATED BLINDLY IN THE VOID.

OTHERS WERE THERE, PASSING THROUGH IN PEACEFUL TIMELESSNESS.

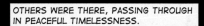

PULLING ME ONCE AGAIN TOWARD EXISTENCE.

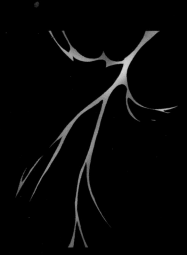

THEN I FELT A FORCE, PULLING ME TOWARD SOMETHING OR SOMEONE.

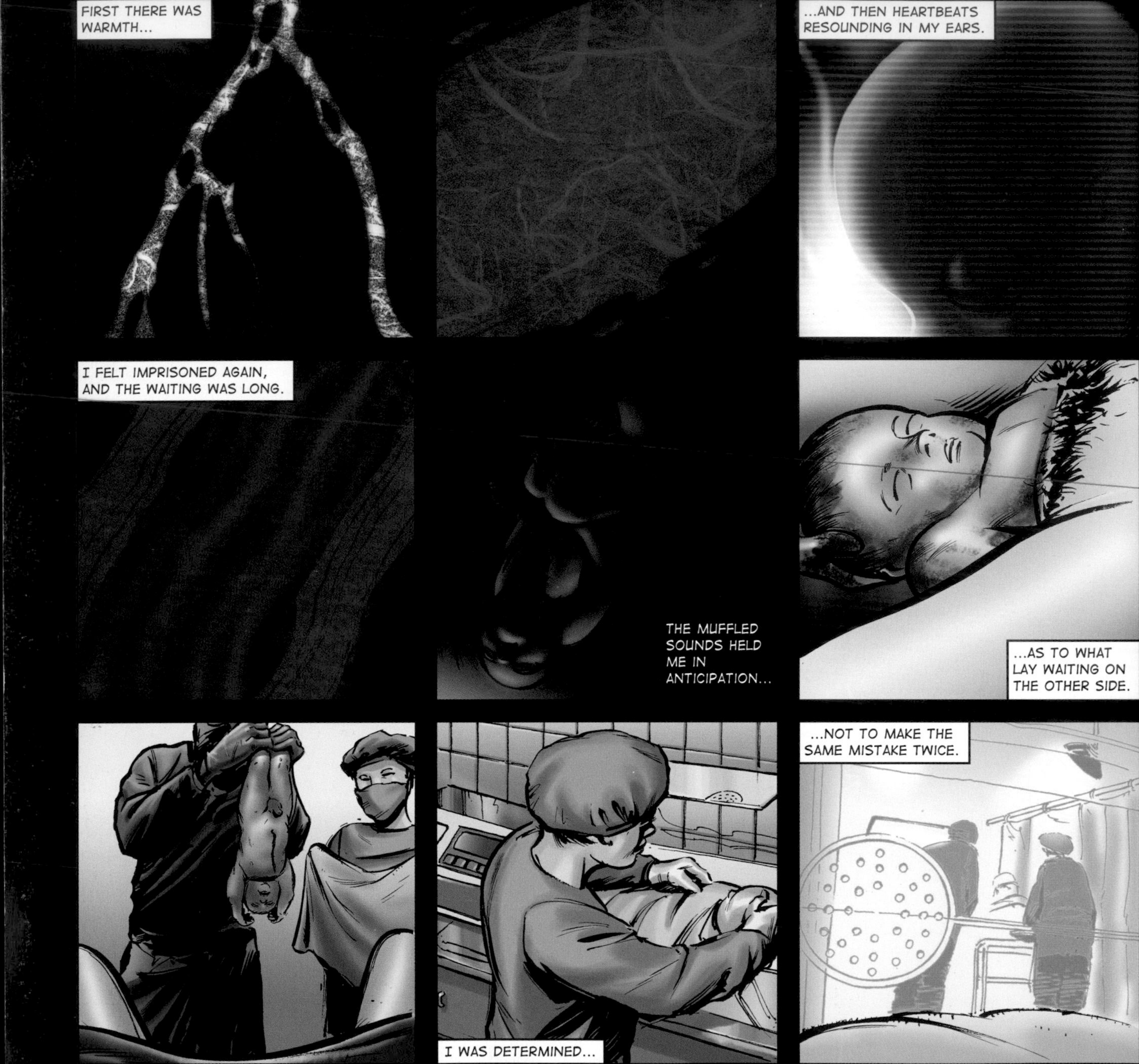
FIRST THERE WAS WARMTH...
...AND THEN HEARTBEATS RESOUNDING IN MY EARS.
I FELT IMPRISONED AGAIN, AND THE WAITING WAS LONG.
THE MUFFLED SOUNDS HELD ME IN ANTICIPATION...
...AS TO WHAT LAY WAITING ON THE OTHER SIDE.
I WAS DETERMINED...
...NOT TO MAKE THE SAME MISTAKE TWICE.

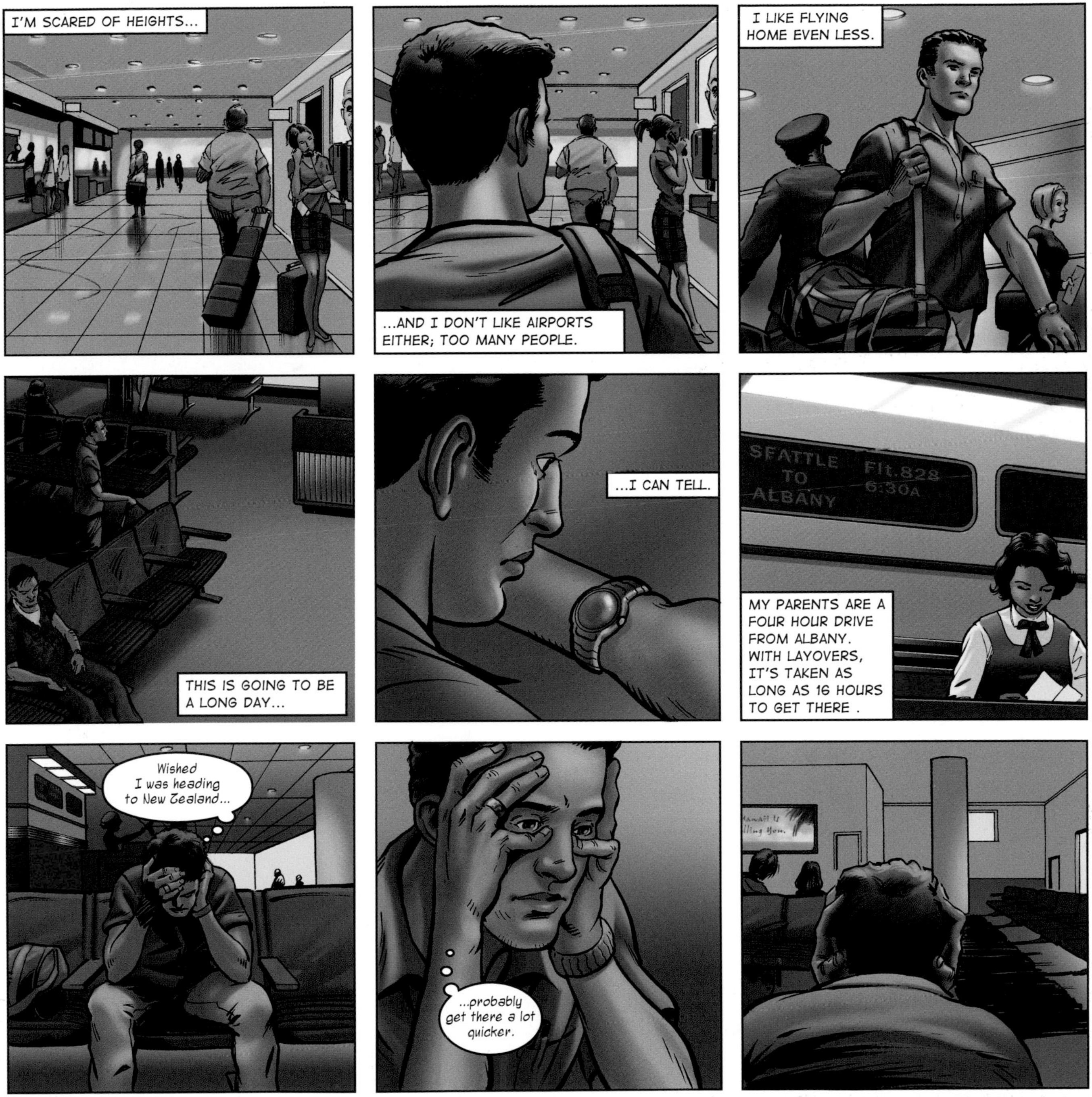
I'M SCARED OF HEIGHTS...
...AND I DON'T LIKE AIRPORTS EITHER; TOO MANY PEOPLE.
I LIKE FLYING HOME EVEN LESS.
THIS IS GOING TO BE A LONG DAY...
...I CAN TELL.
SEATTLE TO ALBANY
Flt.828 6:30A
MY PARENTS ARE A FOUR HOUR DRIVE FROM ALBANY. WITH LAYOVERS, IT'S TAKEN AS LONG AS 16 HOURS TO GET THERE .
Wished I was heading to New Zealand...
...probably get there a lot quicker.

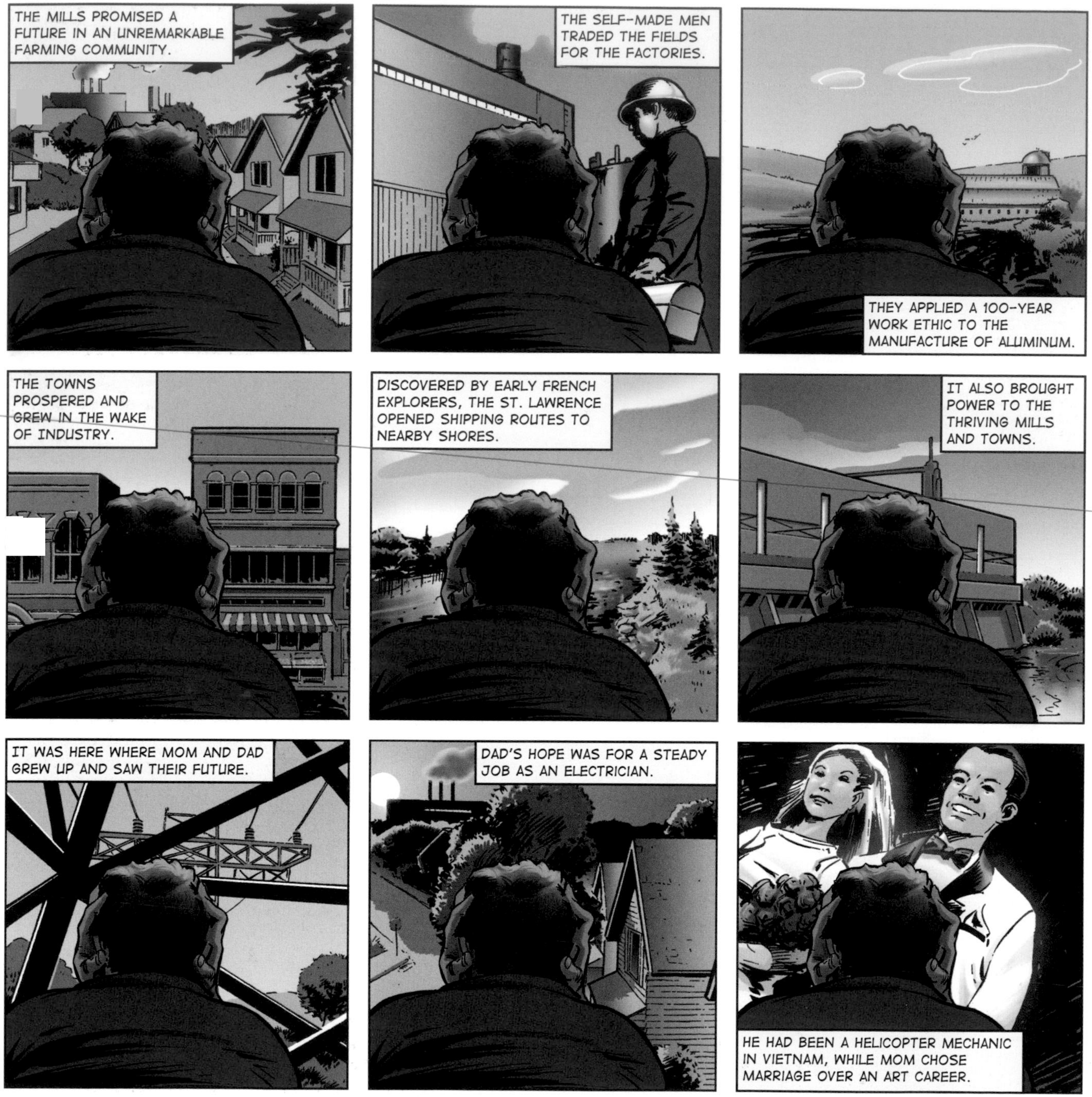
THE MILLS PROMISED A FUTURE IN AN UNREMARKABLE FARMING COMMUNITY.
THE SELF-MADE MEN TRADED THE FIELDS FOR THE FACTORIES.
THEY APPLIED A 100-YEAR WORK ETHIC TO THE MANUFACTURE OF ALUMINUM.
THE TOWNS PROSPERED AND GREW IN THE WAKE OF INDUSTRY.
DISCOVERED BY EARLY FRENCH EXPLORERS, THE ST. LAWRENCE OPENED SHIPPING ROUTES TO NEARBY SHORES.
IT ALSO BROUGHT POWER TO THE THRIVING MILLS AND TOWNS.
IT WAS HERE WHERE MOM AND DAD GREW UP AND SAW THEIR FUTURE.
DAD'S HOPE WAS FOR A STEADY JOB AS AN ELECTRICIAN.
HE HAD BEEN A HELICOPTER MECHANIC IN VIETNAM, WHILE MOM CHOSE MARRIAGE OVER AN ART CAREER.

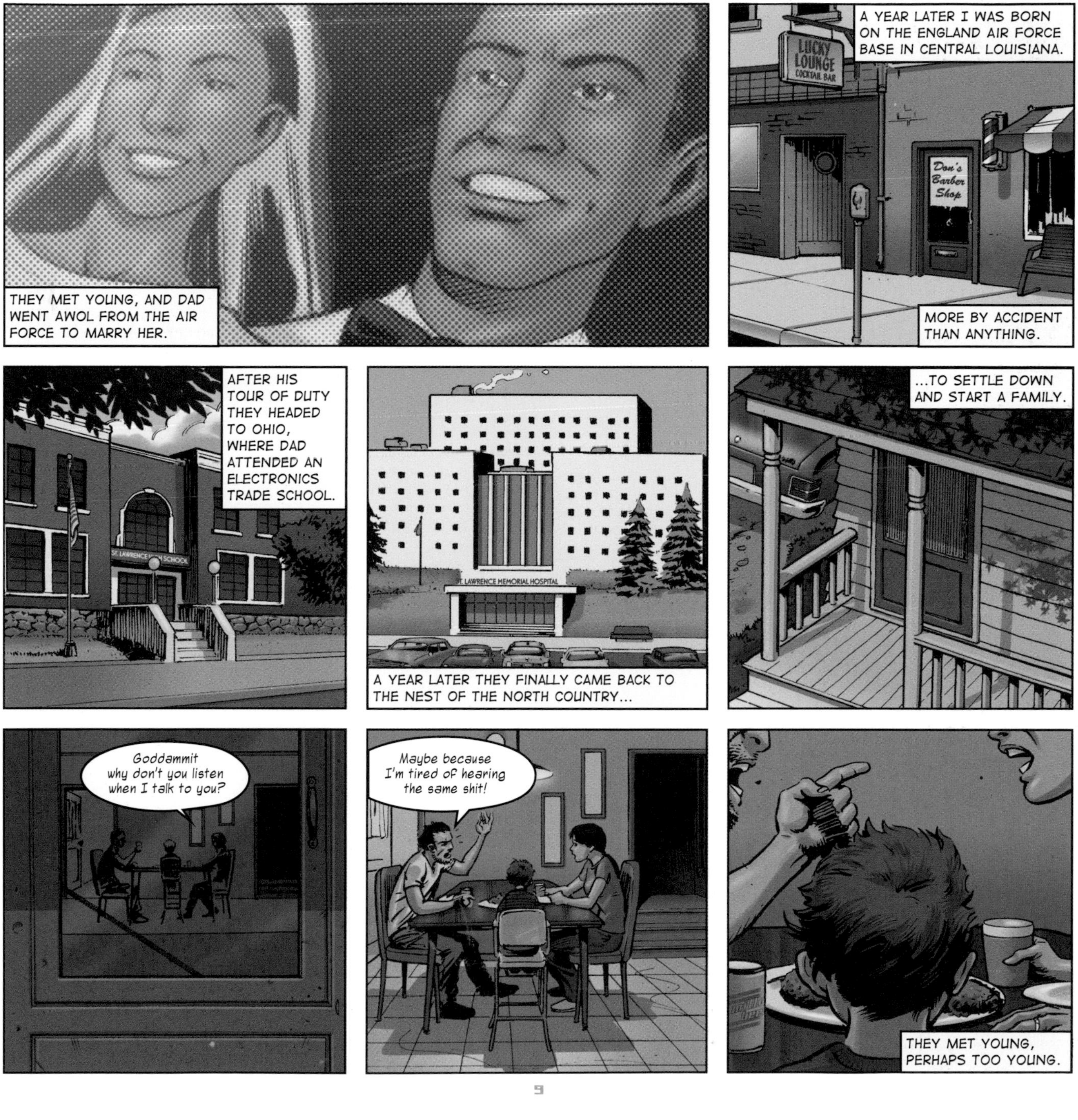
THEY MET YOUNG, AND DAD WENT AWOL FROM THE AIR FORCE TO MARRY HER.
A YEAR LATER I WAS BORN ON THE ENGLAND AIR FORCE BASE IN CENTRAL LOUISIANA.
LUCKY LOUNGE COCKTAIL BAR
Don's Barber Shop
MORE BY ACCIDENT THAN ANYTHING.
AFTER HIS TOUR OF DUTY THEY HEADED TO OHIO, WHERE DAD ATTENDED AN ELECTRONICS TRADE SCHOOL.
ST. LAWRENCE MEMORIAL HOSPITAL
A YEAR LATER THEY FINALLY CAME BACK TO THE NEST OF THE NORTH COUNTRY...
...TO SETTLE DOWN AND START A FAMILY.
Goddammit why don't you listen when I talk to you?
Maybe because I'm tired of hearing the same shit!
THEY MET YOUNG, PERHAPS TOO YOUNG.

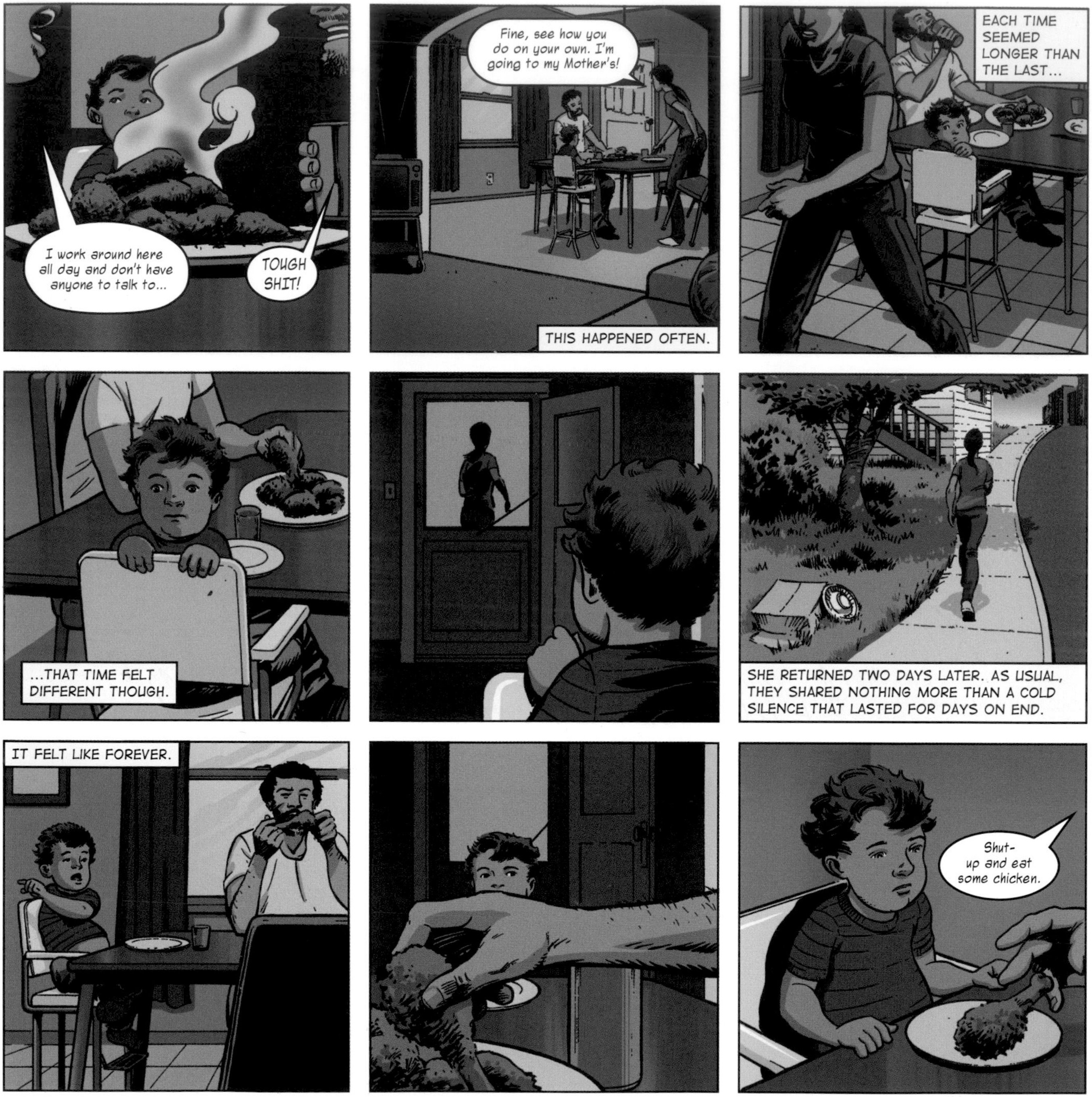
I work around here all day and don't have anyone to talk to...
TOUGH SHIT!
Fine, see how you do on your own. I'm going to my Mother's!
THIS HAPPENED OFTEN.
EACH TIME SEEMED LONGER THAN THE LAST...
...THAT TIME FELT DIFFERENT THOUGH.
SHE RETURNED TWO DAYS LATER. AS USUAL, THEY SHARED NOTHING MORE THAN A COLD SILENCE THAT LASTED FOR DAYS ON END.
IT FELT LIKE FOREVER.
Shut-up and eat some chicken.

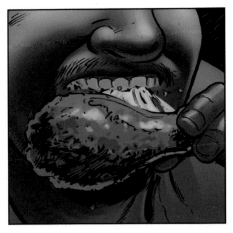

Jesus Christ, what's that smell?

SNIFF SNIFF

What kind of breakfast is that anyway?

Fucking heart-attack-over-easy is what it is.

IT USED TO BE HARDER TO DEAL WITH THIS. TRAVELING HOME I MEAN.

How can people do that to themselves?

BEFORE, I'D HAVE ANXIETY AND NIGHTMARES WHERE WE'RE ALL YELLING AT EACH OTHER WITH THE FORCE OF HURRICANES.

You've got one body, one chance at life...why make such a bad investment so early on?

NOW IT'S JUST ANXIETY.

Glad I got here early.

SOME OF THE DREAMS WOULD BE ABOUT OUR HOUSE...

I'm tired and nervous. I just need to relax.

...ITS VAST INTERIORS ALWAYS IN A HUGE STATE OF DISREPAIR...

...CREAKING AND MOANING UNDER DECADES OF NEGLECT.

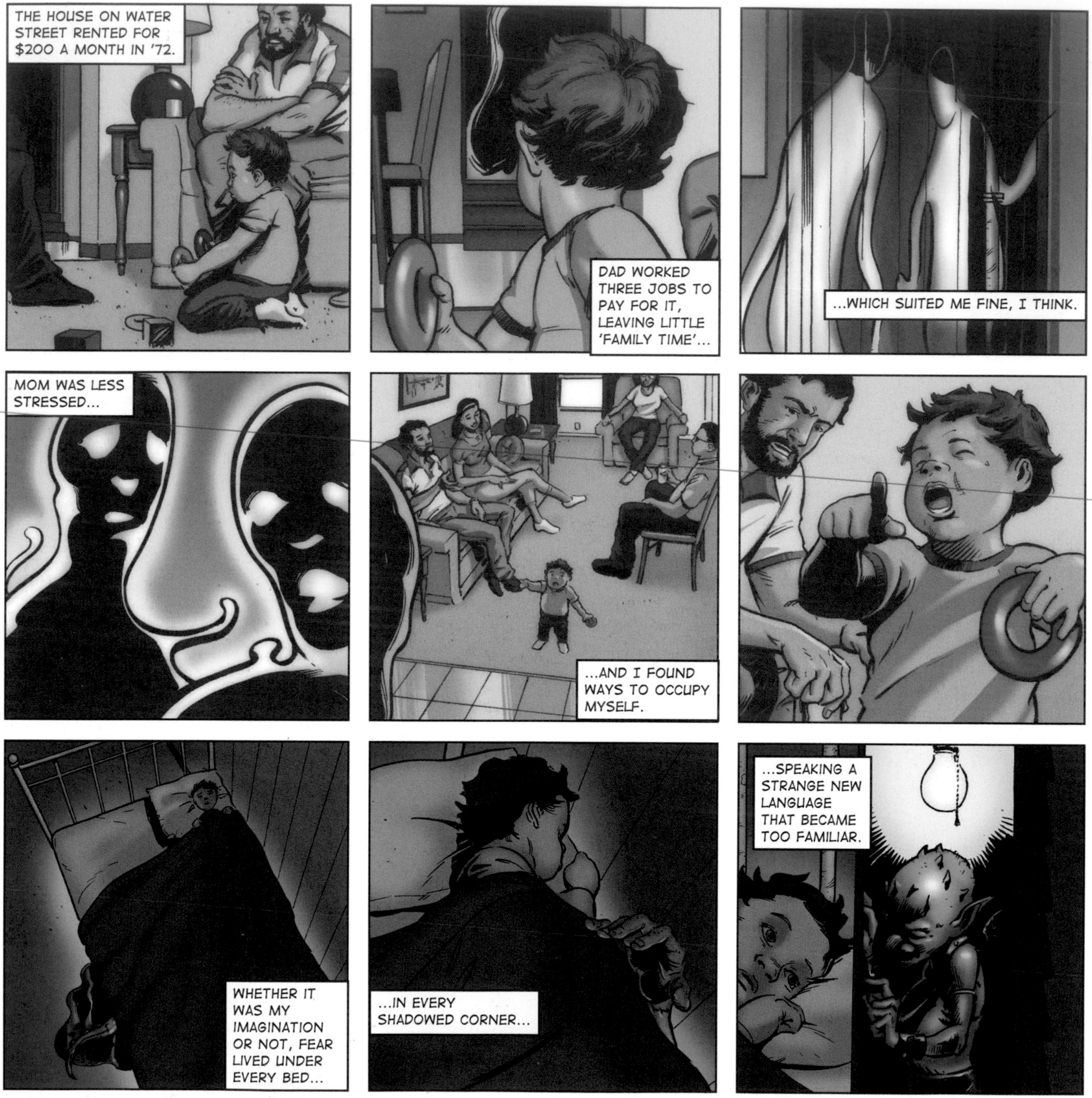
THE HOUSE ON WATER STREET RENTED FOR $200 A MONTH IN '72.
DAD WORKED THREE JOBS TO PAY FOR IT, LEAVING LITTLE 'FAMILY TIME'...
...WHICH SUITED ME FINE, I THINK.
MOM WAS LESS STRESSED...
...AND I FOUND WAYS TO OCCUPY MYSELF.
WHETHER IT WAS MY IMAGINATION OR NOT, FEAR LIVED UNDER EVERY BED...
...IN EVERY SHADOWED CORNER...
...SPEAKING A STRANGE NEW LANGUAGE THAT BECAME TOO FAMILIAR.

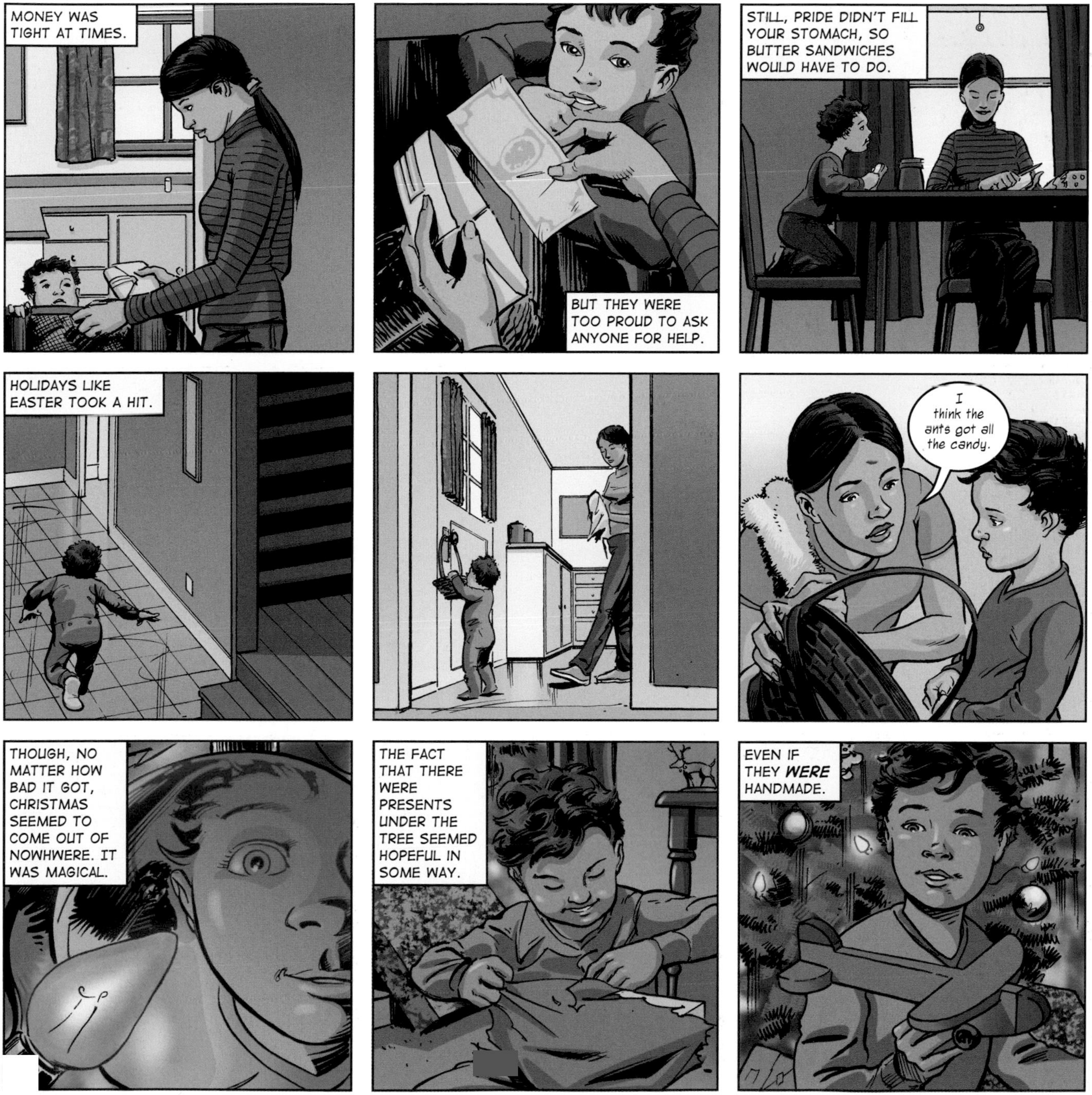
MONEY WAS TIGHT AT TIMES.
BUT THEY WERE TOO PROUD TO ASK ANYONE FOR HELP.
STILL, PRIDE DIDN'T FILL YOUR STOMACH, SO BUTTER SANDWICHES WOULD HAVE TO DO.
HOLIDAYS LIKE EASTER TOOK A HIT.
I think the ants got all the candy.
THOUGH, NO MATTER HOW BAD IT GOT, CHRISTMAS SEEMED TO COME OUT OF NOWHWERE. IT WAS MAGICAL.
THE FACT THAT THERE WERE PRESENTS UNDER THE TREE SEEMED HOPEFUL IN SOME WAY.
EVEN IF THEY ***WERE*** HANDMADE.

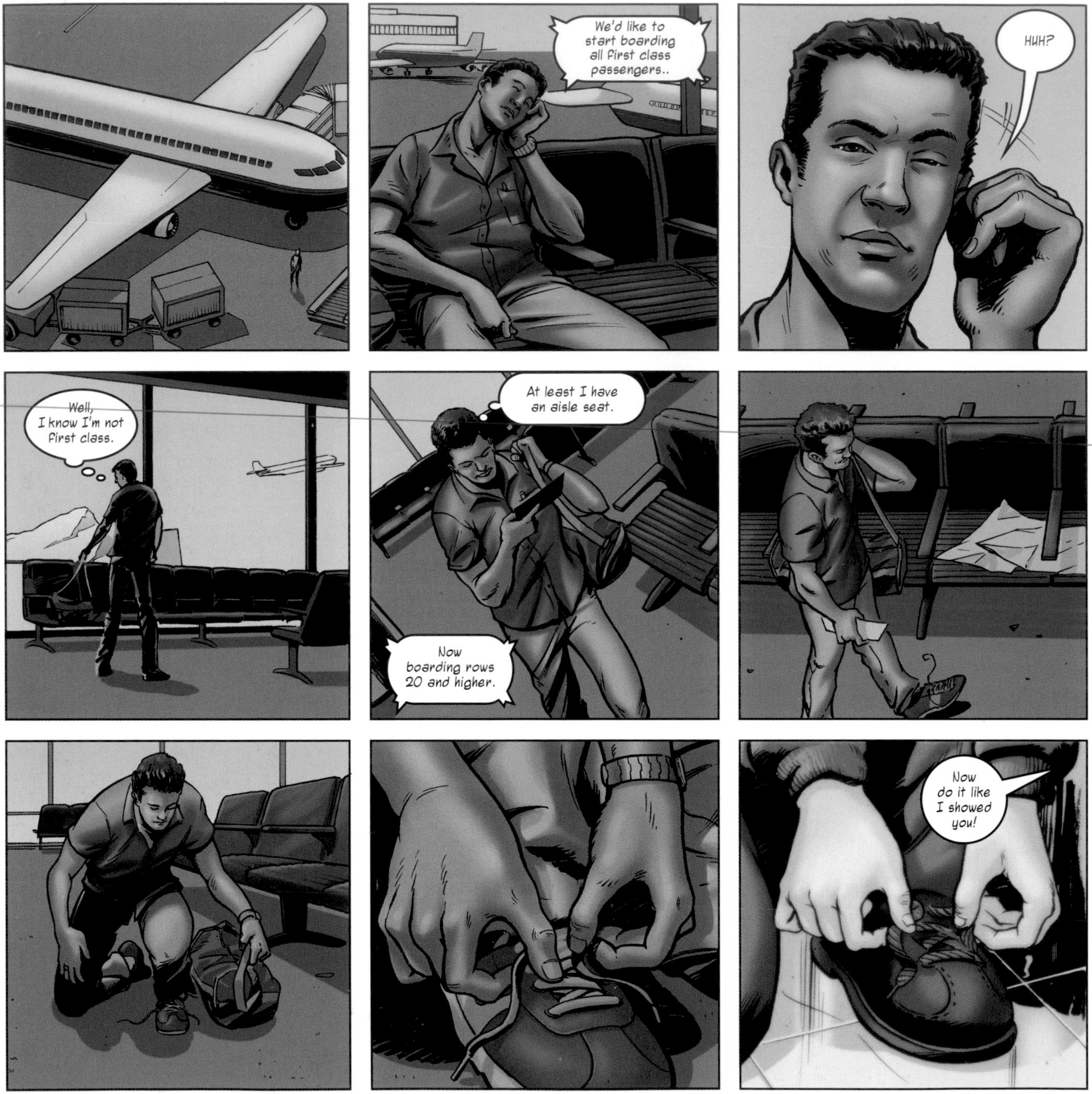
We'd like to start boarding all first class passengers..
HUH?
Well, I know I'm not first class.
At least I have an aisle seat.
Now boarding rows 20 and higher.
Now do it like I showed you!

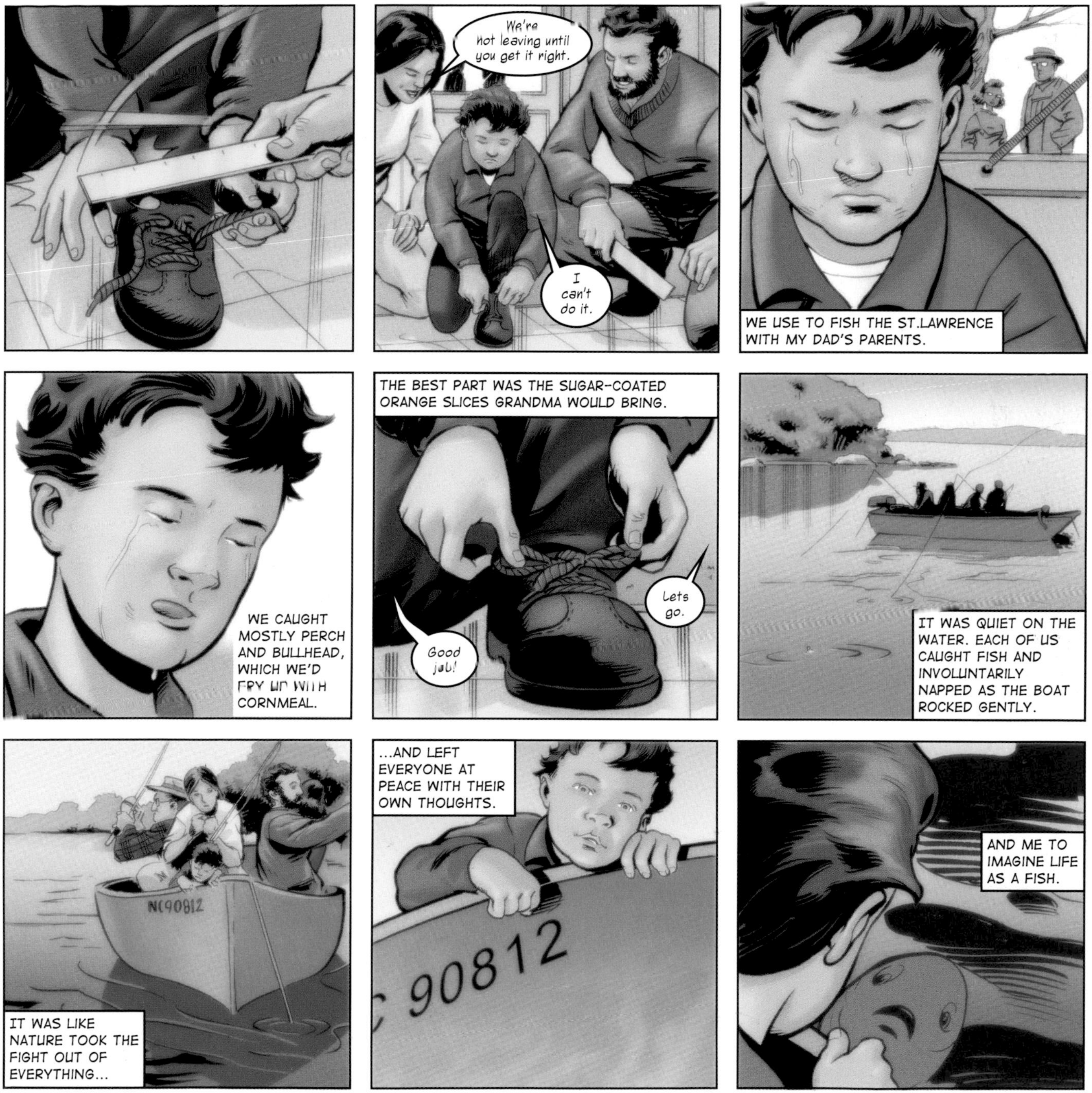
We're not leaving until you get it right.
I can't do it.
WE USE TO FISH THE ST.LAWRENCE WITH MY DAD'S PARENTS.
WE CAUGHT MOSTLY PERCH AND BULLHEAD, WHICH WE'D FRY UP WITH CORNMEAL.
THE BEST PART WAS THE SUGAR-COATED ORANGE SLICES GRANDMA WOULD BRING.
Good job!
Lets go.
IT WAS QUIET ON THE WATER. EACH OF US CAUGHT FISH AND INVOLUNTARILY NAPPED AS THE BOAT ROCKED GENTLY.
IT WAS LIKE NATURE TOOK THE FIGHT OUT OF EVERYTHING...
NC90812
...AND LEFT EVERYONE AT PEACE WITH THEIR OWN THOUGHTS.
C 90812
AND ME TO IMAGINE LIFE AS A FISH.

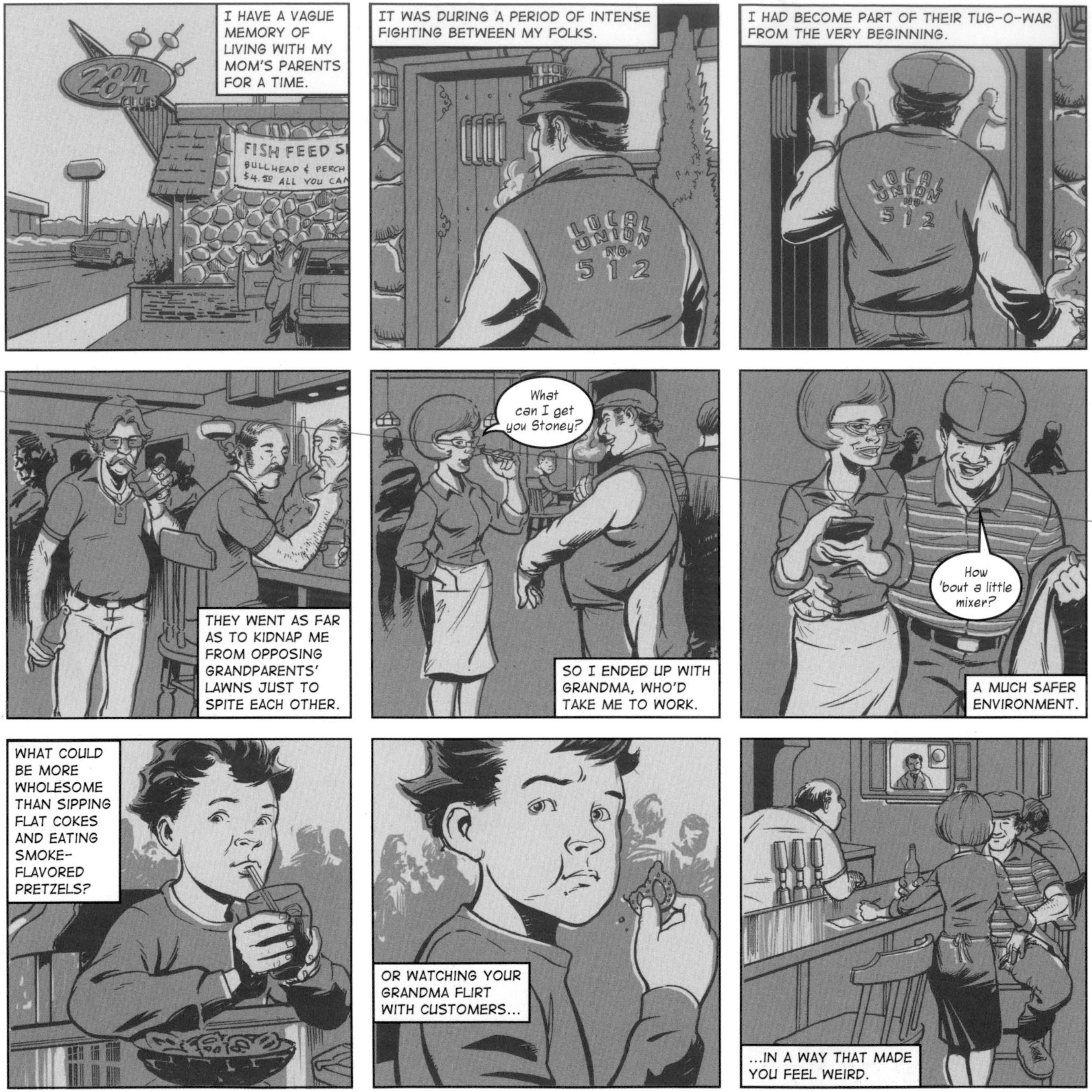
I HAVE A VAGUE MEMORY OF LIVING WITH MY MOM'S PARENTS FOR A TIME.
284 CLUB
FISH FEED S
BULLHEAD & PERCH
$4.50 ALL YOU CAN
IT WAS DURING A PERIOD OF INTENSE FIGHTING BETWEEN MY FOLKS.
LOCAL UNION NO. 512
I HAD BECOME PART OF THEIR TUG-O-WAR FROM THE VERY BEGINNING.
LOCAL UNION NO. 512
THEY WENT AS FAR AS TO KIDNAP ME FROM OPPOSING GRANDPARENTS' LAWNS JUST TO SPITE EACH OTHER.
What can I get you Stoney?
SO I ENDED UP WITH GRANDMA, WHO'D TAKE ME TO WORK.
How 'bout a little mixer?
A MUCH SAFER ENVIRONMENT.
WHAT COULD BE MORE WHOLESOME THAN SIPPING FLAT COKES AND EATING SMOKE-FLAVORED PRETZELS?
OR WATCHING YOUR GRANDMA FLIRT WITH CUSTOMERS...
...IN A WAY THAT MADE YOU FEEL WEIRD.

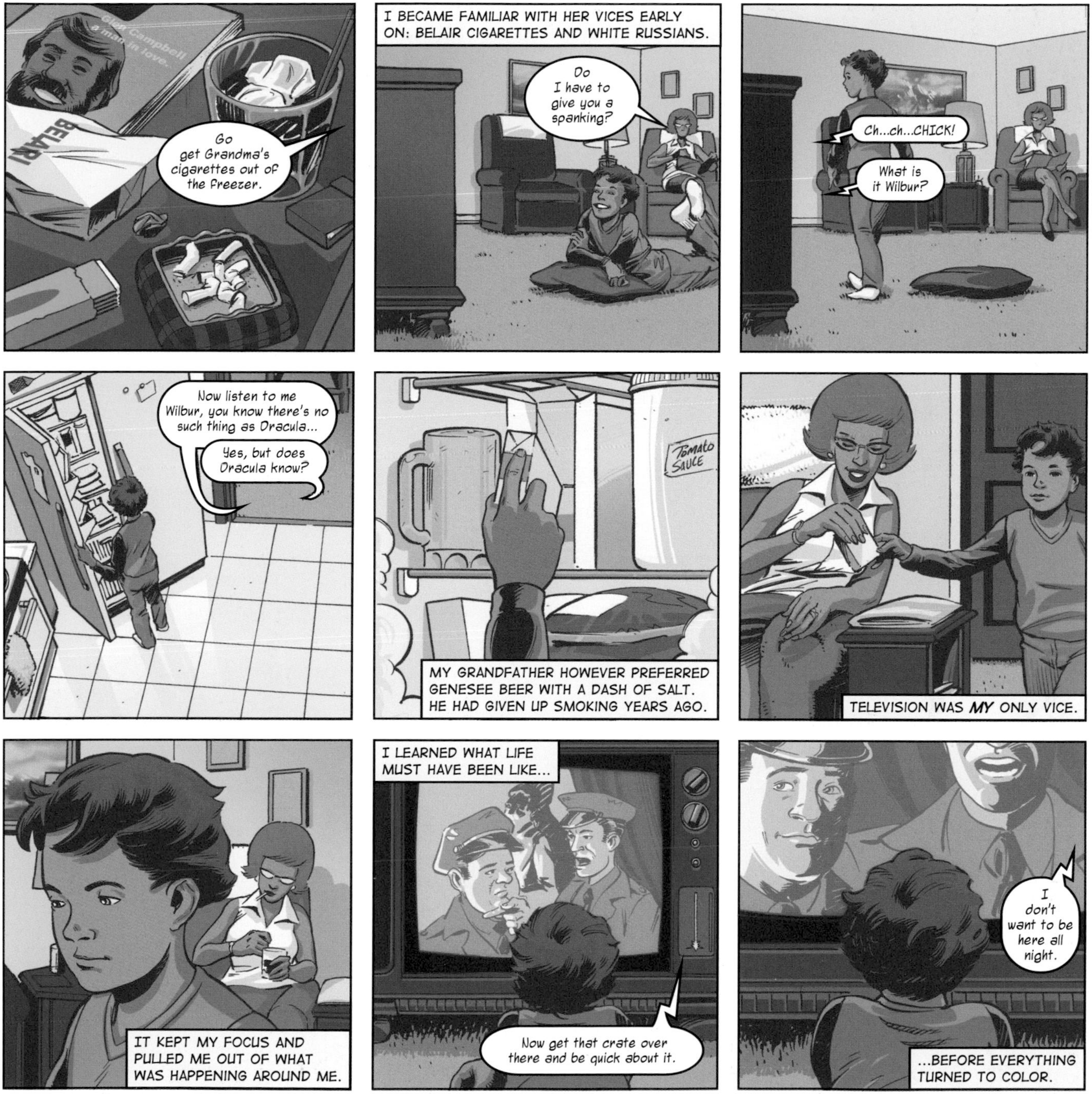
Go get Grandma's cigarettes out of the freezer.
I BECAME FAMILIAR WITH HER VICES EARLY ON: BELAIR CIGARETTES AND WHITE RUSSIANS.
Do I have to give you a spanking?
Ch...ch...CHICK!
What is it Wilbur?
Now listen to me Wilbur, you know there's no such thing as Dracula...
Yes, but does Dracula know?
Tomato Sauce
MY GRANDFATHER HOWEVER PREFERRED GENESEE BEER WITH A DASH OF SALT. HE HAD GIVEN UP SMOKING YEARS AGO.
TELEVISION WAS *MY* ONLY VICE.
IT KEPT MY FOCUS AND PULLED ME OUT OF WHAT WAS HAPPENING AROUND ME.
I LEARNED WHAT LIFE MUST HAVE BEEN LIKE...
Now get that crate over there and be quick about it.
I don't want to be here all night.
...BEFORE EVERYTHING TURNED TO COLOR.

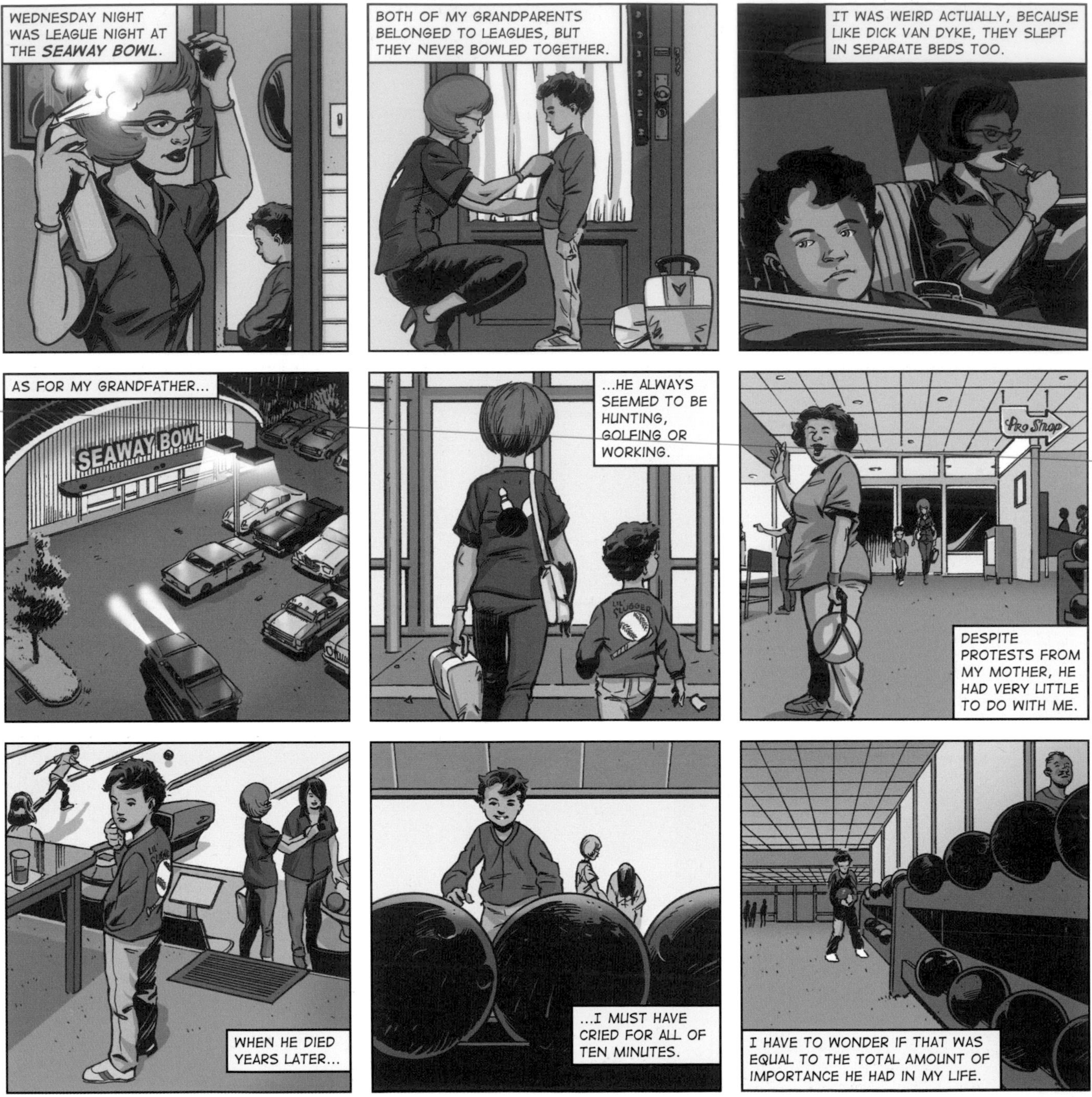
WEDNESDAY NIGHT WAS LEAGUE NIGHT AT THE ***SEAWAY BOWL***.
BOTH OF MY GRANDPARENTS BELONGED TO LEAGUES, BUT THEY NEVER BOWLED TOGETHER.
IT WAS WEIRD ACTUALLY, BECAUSE LIKE DICK VAN DYKE, THEY SLEPT IN SEPARATE BEDS TOO.
AS FOR MY GRANDFATHER...
SEAWAY BOWL
...HE ALWAYS SEEMED TO BE HUNTING, GOLFING OR WORKING.
LIL' SLUGGER
PRO SHOP
DESPITE PROTESTS FROM MY MOTHER, HE HAD VERY LITTLE TO DO WITH ME.
WHEN HE DIED YEARS LATER...
...I MUST HAVE CRIED FOR ALL OF TEN MINUTES.
I HAVE TO WONDER IF THAT WAS EQUAL TO THE TOTAL AMOUNT OF IMPORTANCE HE HAD IN MY LIFE.

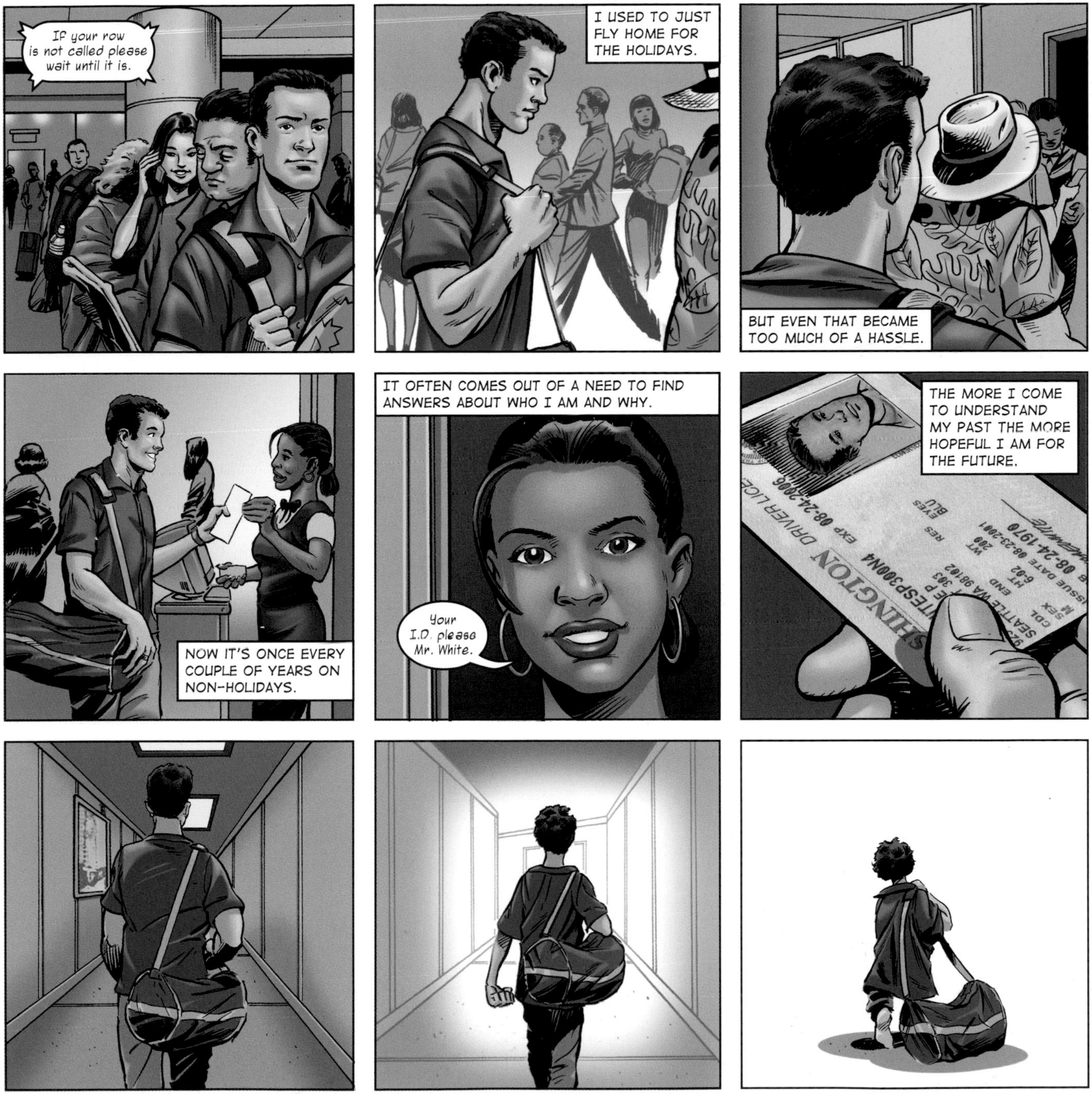
If your row is not called please wait until it is.
I USED TO JUST FLY HOME FOR THE HOLIDAYS.
BUT EVEN THAT BECAME TOO MUCH OF A HASSLE.
NOW IT'S ONCE EVERY COUPLE OF YEARS ON NON-HOLIDAYS.
IT OFTEN COMES OUT OF A NEED TO FIND ANSWERS ABOUT WHO I AM AND WHY.
Your I.D. please Mr. White.
THE MORE I COME TO UNDERSTAND MY PAST THE MORE HOPEFUL I AM FOR THE FUTURE.

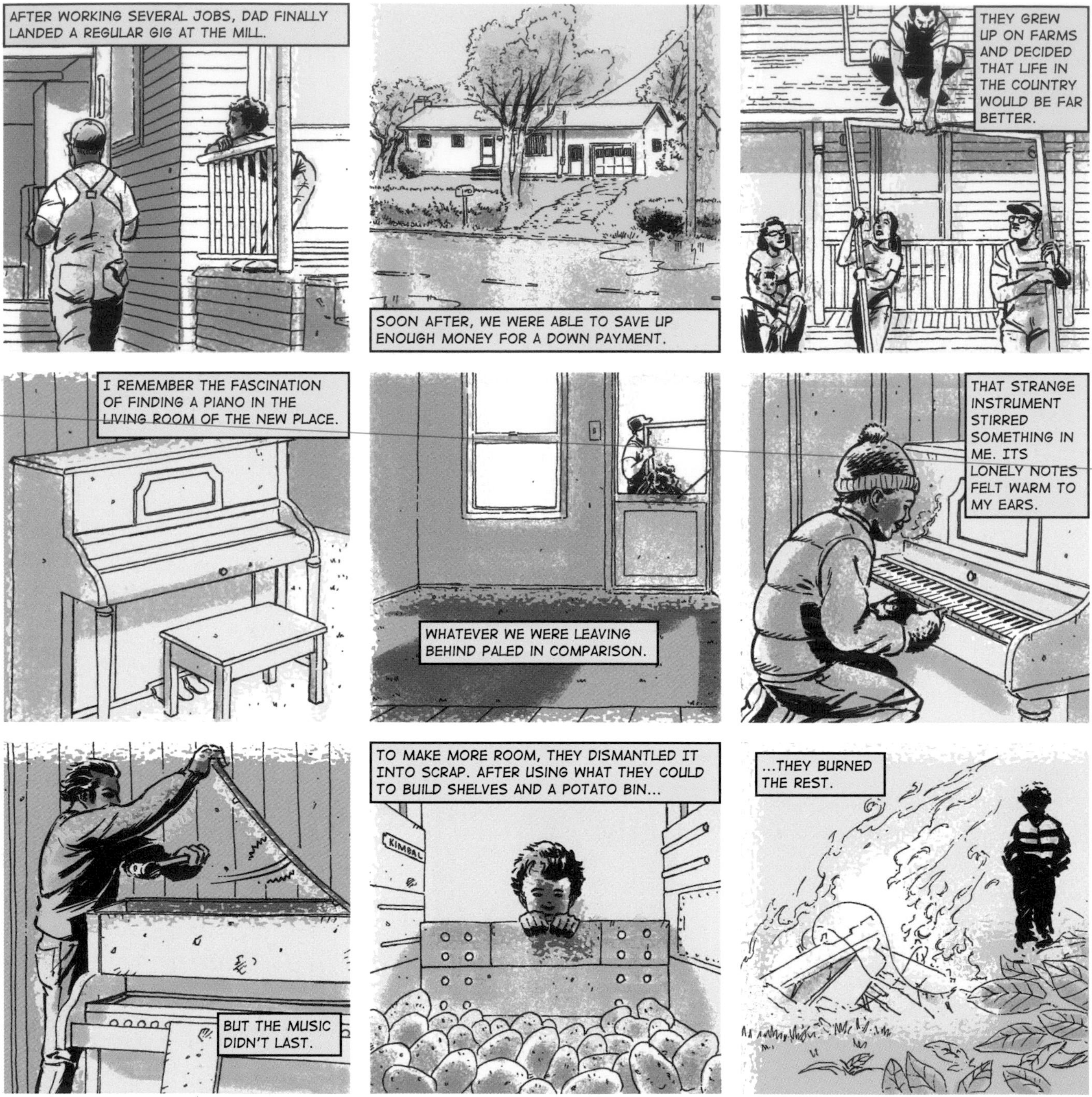
AFTER WORKING SEVERAL JOBS, DAD FINALLY LANDED A REGULAR GIG AT THE MILL.
SOON AFTER, WE WERE ABLE TO SAVE UP ENOUGH MONEY FOR A DOWN PAYMENT.
THEY GREW UP ON FARMS AND DECIDED THAT LIFE IN THE COUNTRY WOULD BE FAR BETTER.
I REMEMBER THE FASCINATION OF FINDING A PIANO IN THE LIVING ROOM OF THE NEW PLACE.
WHATEVER WE WERE LEAVING BEHIND PALED IN COMPARISON.
THAT STRANGE INSTRUMENT STIRRED SOMETHING IN ME. ITS LONELY NOTES FELT WARM TO MY EARS.
BUT THE MUSIC DIDN'T LAST.
TO MAKE MORE ROOM, THEY DISMANTLED IT INTO SCRAP. AFTER USING WHAT THEY COULD TO BUILD SHELVES AND A POTATO BIN...
KIMBAL
...THEY BURNED THE REST.

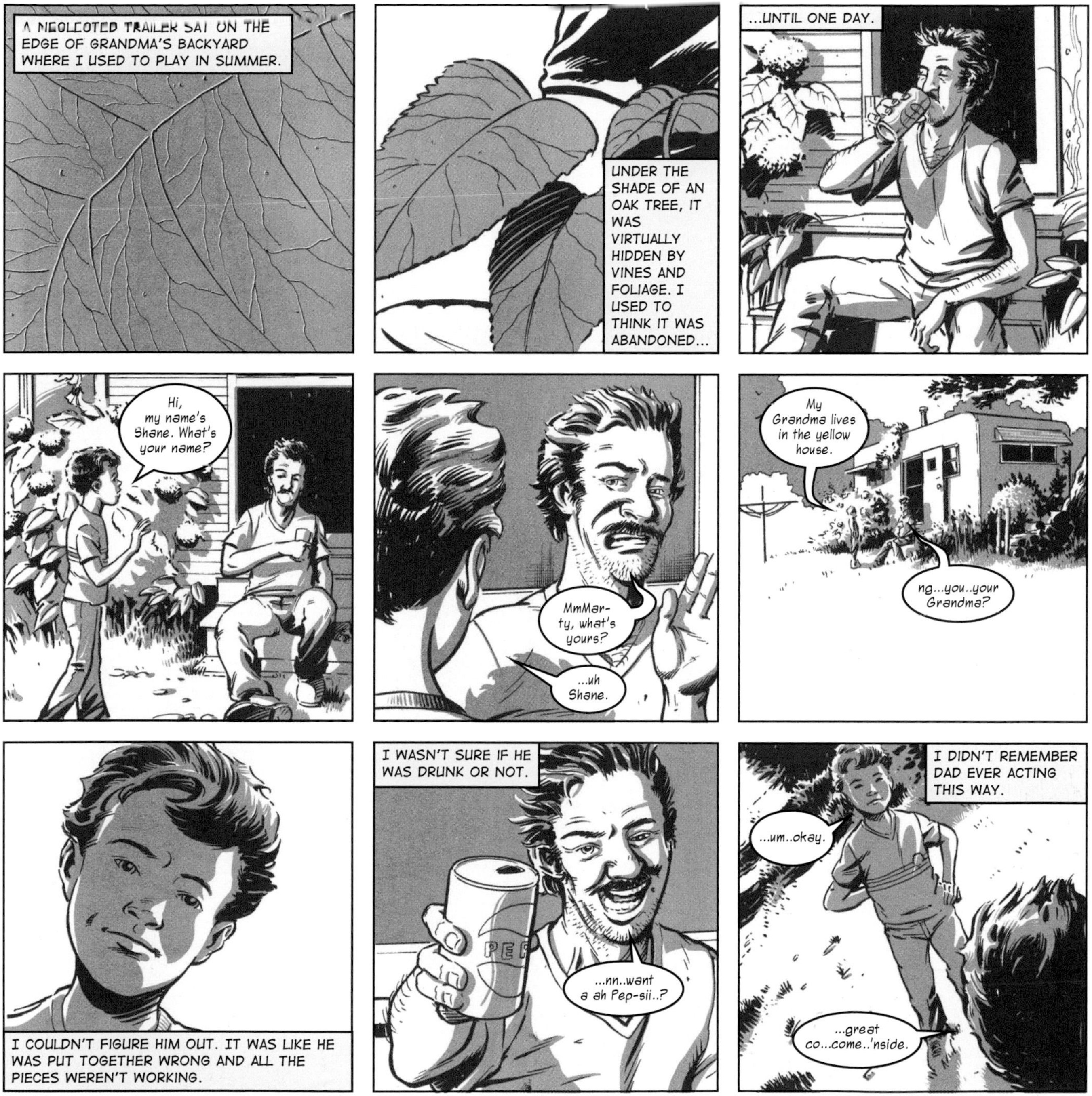
A NEGLECTED TRAILER SAT ON THE EDGE OF GRANDMA'S BACKYARD WHERE I USED TO PLAY IN SUMMER.
UNDER THE SHADE OF AN OAK TREE, IT WAS VIRTUALLY HIDDEN BY VINES AND FOLIAGE. I USED TO THINK IT WAS ABANDONED...
...UNTIL ONE DAY.
Hi, my name's Shane. What's your name?
MmMar-ty, what's yours?
...uh Shane.
My Grandma lives in the yellow house.
ng...you..your Grandma?
I COULDN'T FIGURE HIM OUT. IT WAS LIKE HE WAS PUT TOGETHER WRONG AND ALL THE PIECES WEREN'T WORKING.
I WASN'T SURE IF HE WAS DRUNK OR NOT.
PEP
...nn..want a ah Pep-sii..?
I DIDN'T REMEMBER DAD EVER ACTING THIS WAY.
...um..okay.
...great co...come..'nside.

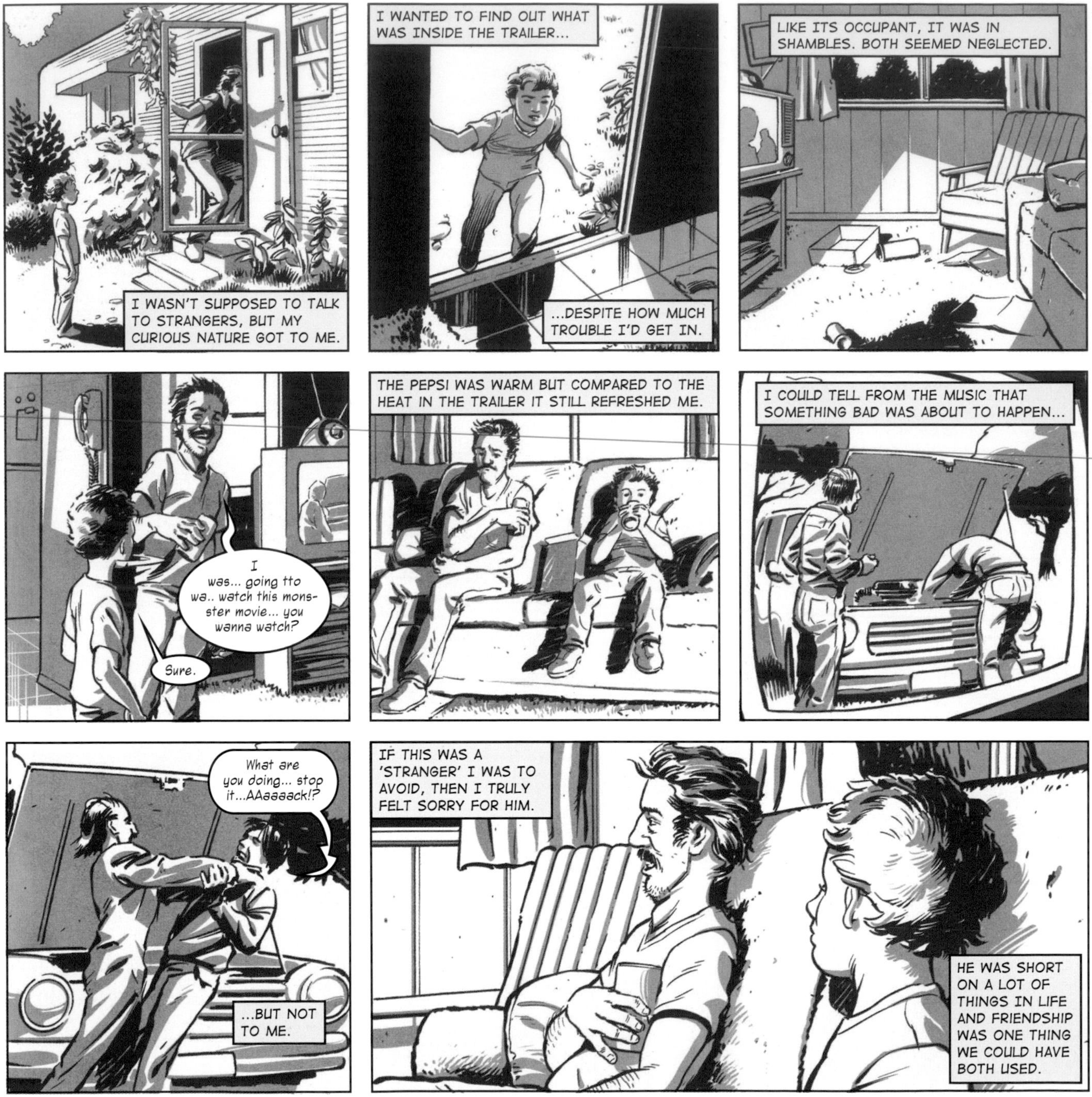
I WASN'T SUPPOSED TO TALK TO STRANGERS, BUT MY CURIOUS NATURE GOT TO ME.
I WANTED TO FIND OUT WHAT WAS INSIDE THE TRAILER...
...DESPITE HOW MUCH TROUBLE I'D GET IN.
LIKE ITS OCCUPANT, IT WAS IN SHAMBLES. BOTH SEEMED NEGLECTED.
I was... going tto wa.. watch this monster movie... you wanna watch?
Sure.
THE PEPSI WAS WARM BUT COMPARED TO THE HEAT IN THE TRAILER IT STILL REFRESHED ME.
I COULD TELL FROM THE MUSIC THAT SOMETHING BAD WAS ABOUT TO HAPPEN...
What are you doing... stop it...AAaaaack!?
...BUT NOT TO ME.
IF THIS WAS A 'STRANGER' I WAS TO AVOID, THEN I TRULY FELT SORRY FOR HIM.
HE WAS SHORT ON A LOT OF THINGS IN LIFE AND FRIENDSHIP WAS ONE THING WE COULD HAVE BOTH USED.

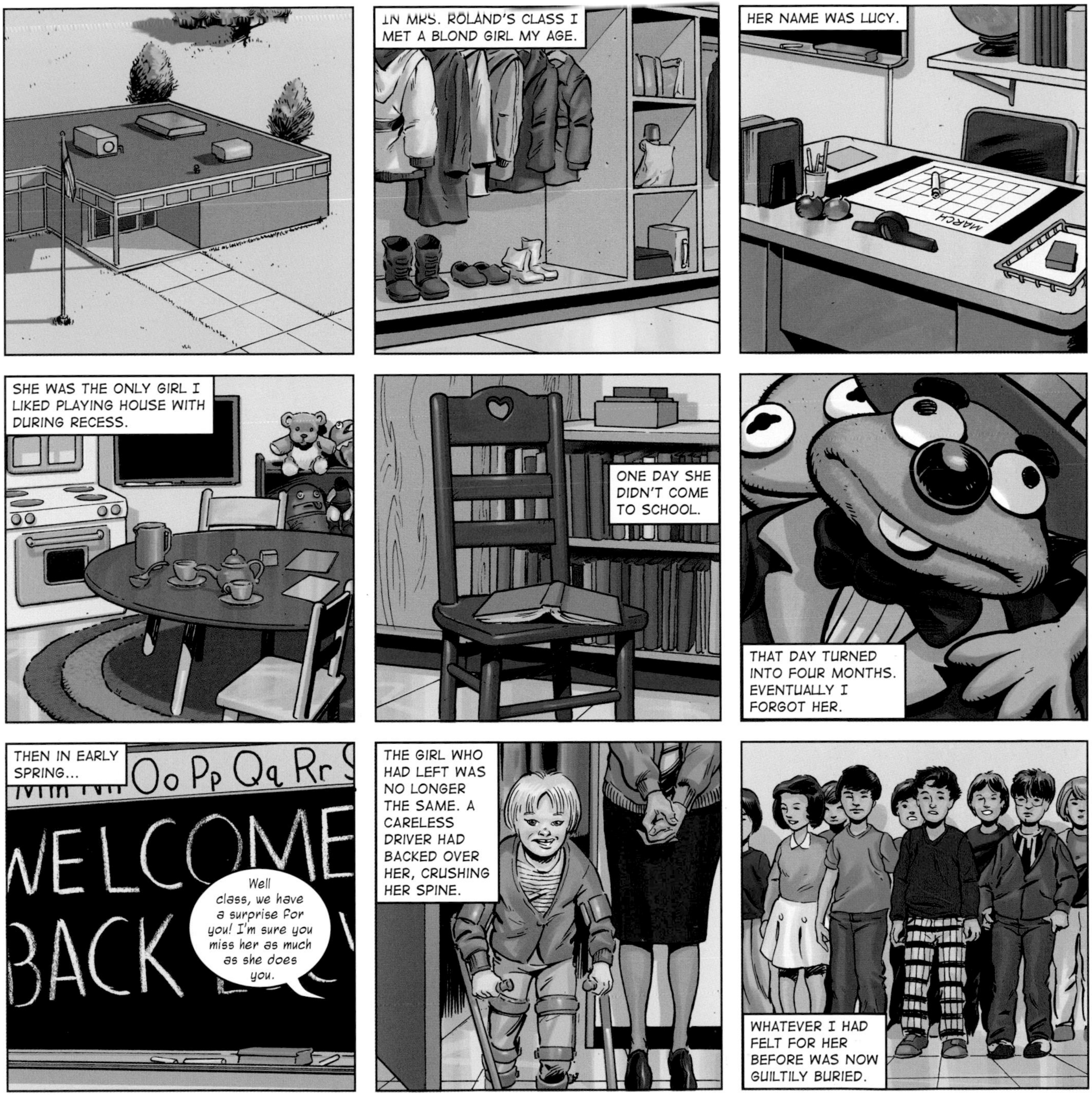
IN MRS. ROLAND'S CLASS I MET A BLOND GIRL MY AGE.
HER NAME WAS LUCY.
MARCH
SHE WAS THE ONLY GIRL I LIKED PLAYING HOUSE WITH DURING RECESS.
ONE DAY SHE DIDN'T COME TO SCHOOL.
THAT DAY TURNED INTO FOUR MONTHS. EVENTUALLY I FORGOT HER.
THEN IN EARLY SPRING...
Oo Pp Qq Rr
WELCOME
BACK
Well class, we have a surprise for you! I'm sure you miss her as much as she does you.
THE GIRL WHO HAD LEFT WAS NO LONGER THE SAME. A CARELESS DRIVER HAD BACKED OVER HER, CRUSHING HER SPINE.
WHATEVER I HAD FELT FOR HER BEFORE WAS NOW GUILTILY BURIED.

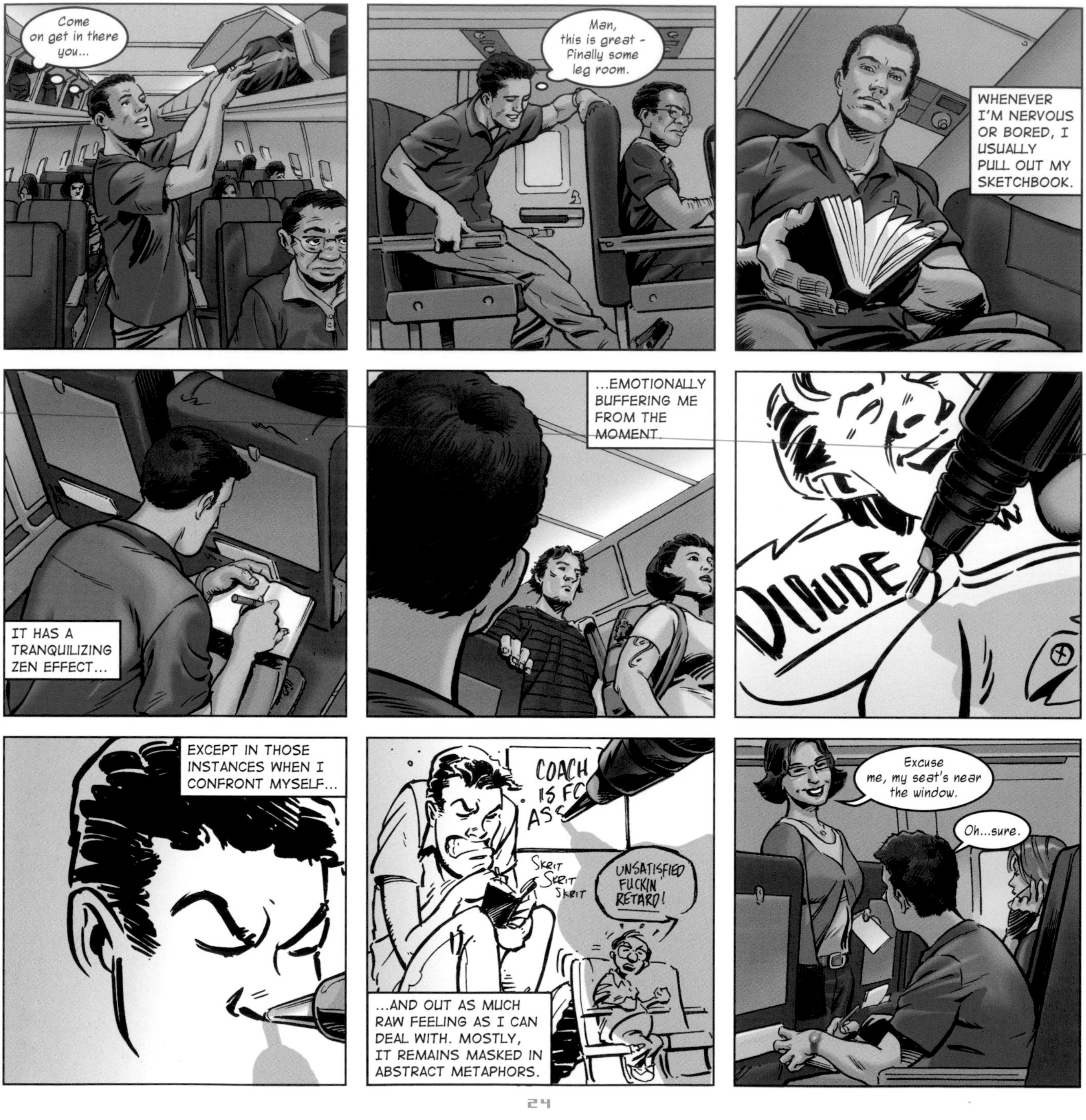

Come on get in there you...
Man, this is great - finally some leg room.
WHENEVER I'M NERVOUS OR BORED, I USUALLY PULL OUT MY SKETCHBOOK.
IT HAS A TRANQUILIZING ZEN EFFECT...
...EMOTIONALLY BUFFERING ME FROM THE MOMENT.
DUUDE
EXCEPT IN THOSE INSTANCES WHEN I CONFRONT MYSELF...
COACH IS FO AS
SKRIT SKRIT SKRIT
UNSATISFIED FUCKIN' RETARD!
...AND OUT AS MUCH RAW FEELING AS I CAN DEAL WITH. MOSTLY, IT REMAINS MASKED IN ABSTRACT METAPHORS.
Excuse me, my seat's near the window.
Oh...sure.

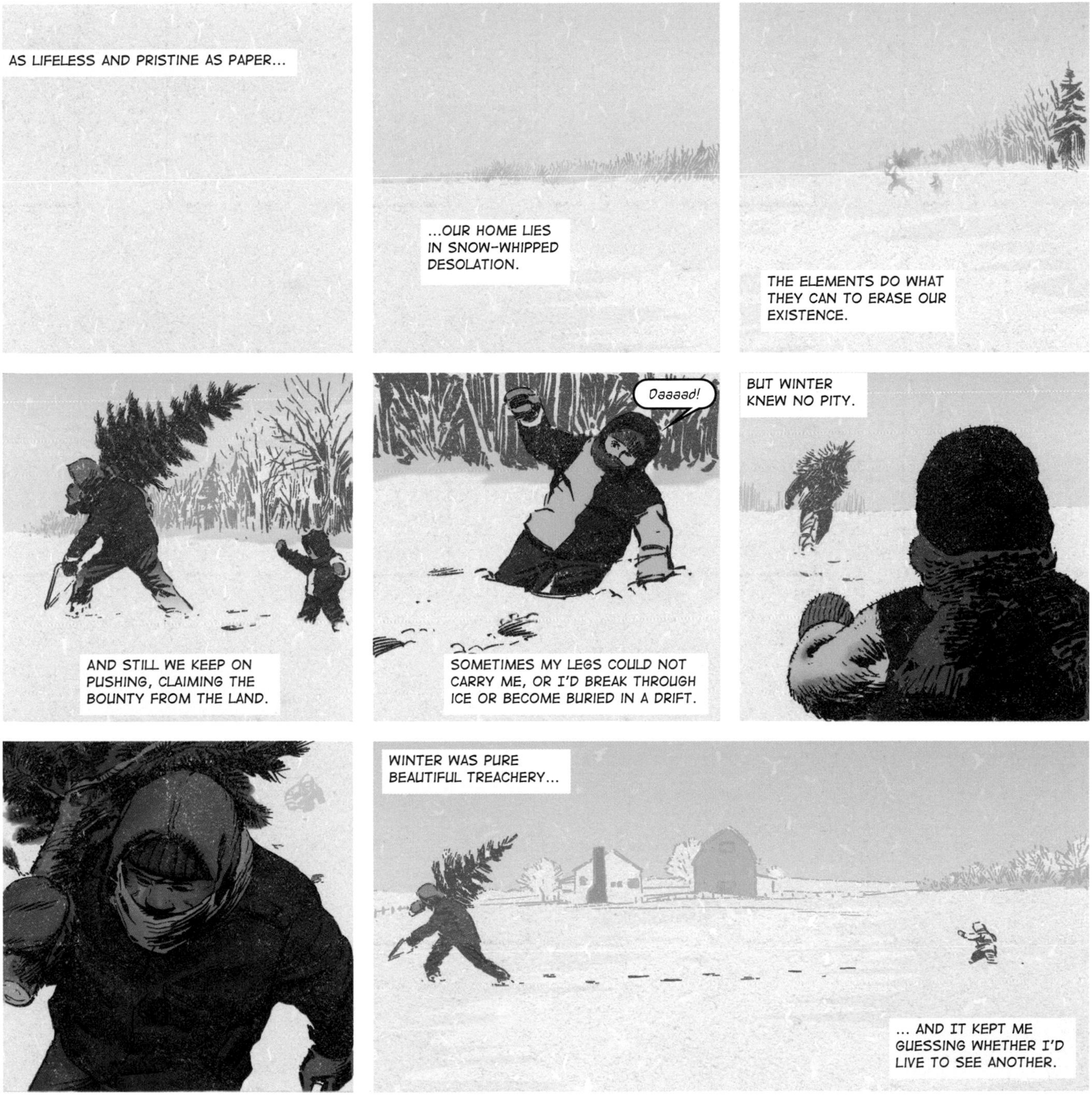
AS LIFELESS AND PRISTINE AS PAPER...
...OUR HOME LIES IN SNOW-WHIPPED DESOLATION.
THE ELEMENTS DO WHAT THEY CAN TO ERASE OUR EXISTENCE.
AND STILL WE KEEP ON PUSHING, CLAIMING THE BOUNTY FROM THE LAND.
Daaaad!
SOMETIMES MY LEGS COULD NOT CARRY ME, OR I'D BREAK THROUGH ICE OR BECOME BURIED IN A DRIFT.
BUT WINTER KNEW NO PITY.
WINTER WAS PURE BEAUTIFUL TREACHERY...
... AND IT KEPT ME GUESSING WHETHER I'D LIVE TO SEE ANOTHER.

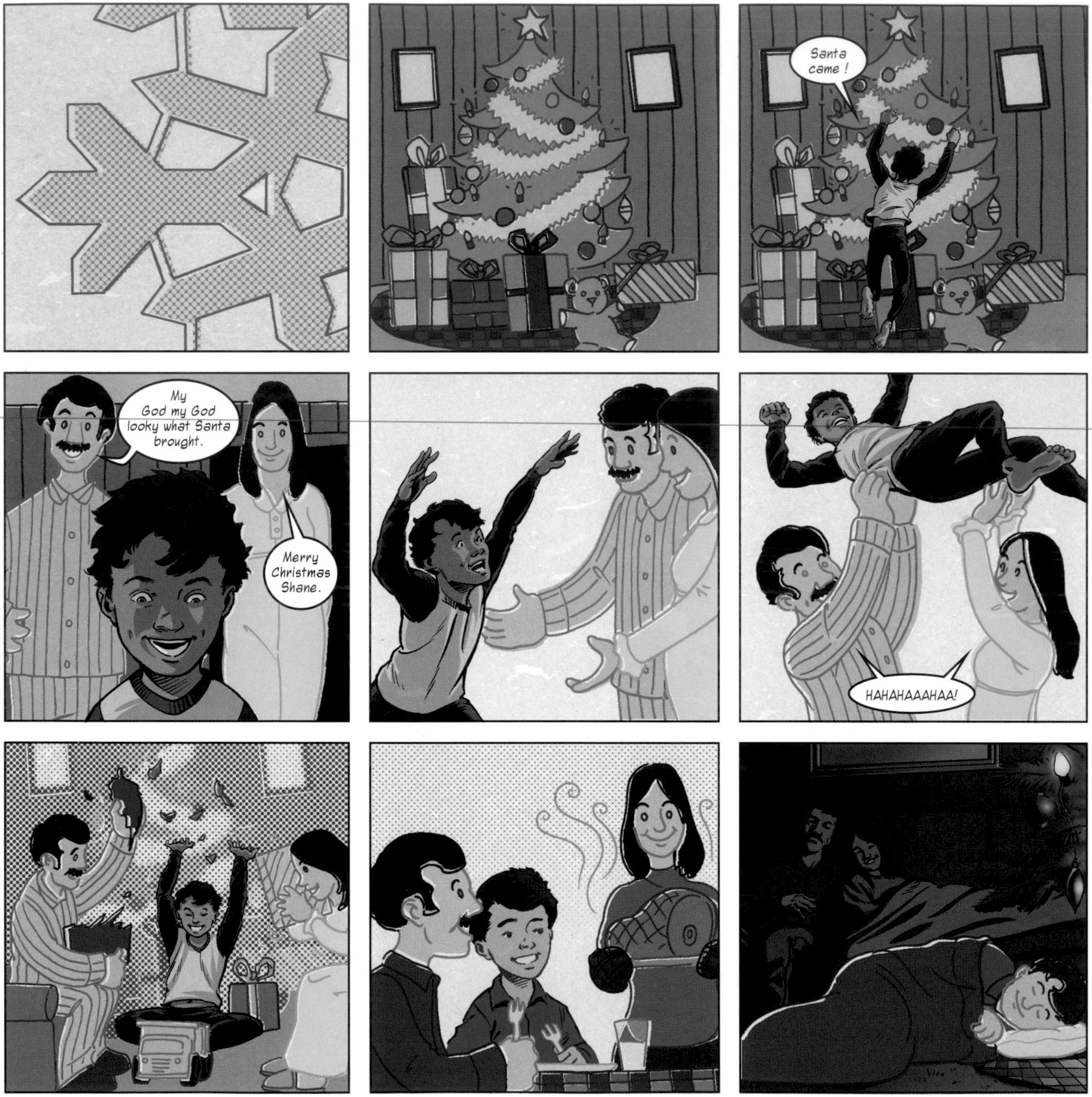
Santa came !
My God my God looky what Santa brought.
Merry Christmas Shane.
HAHAHAAAHAA!

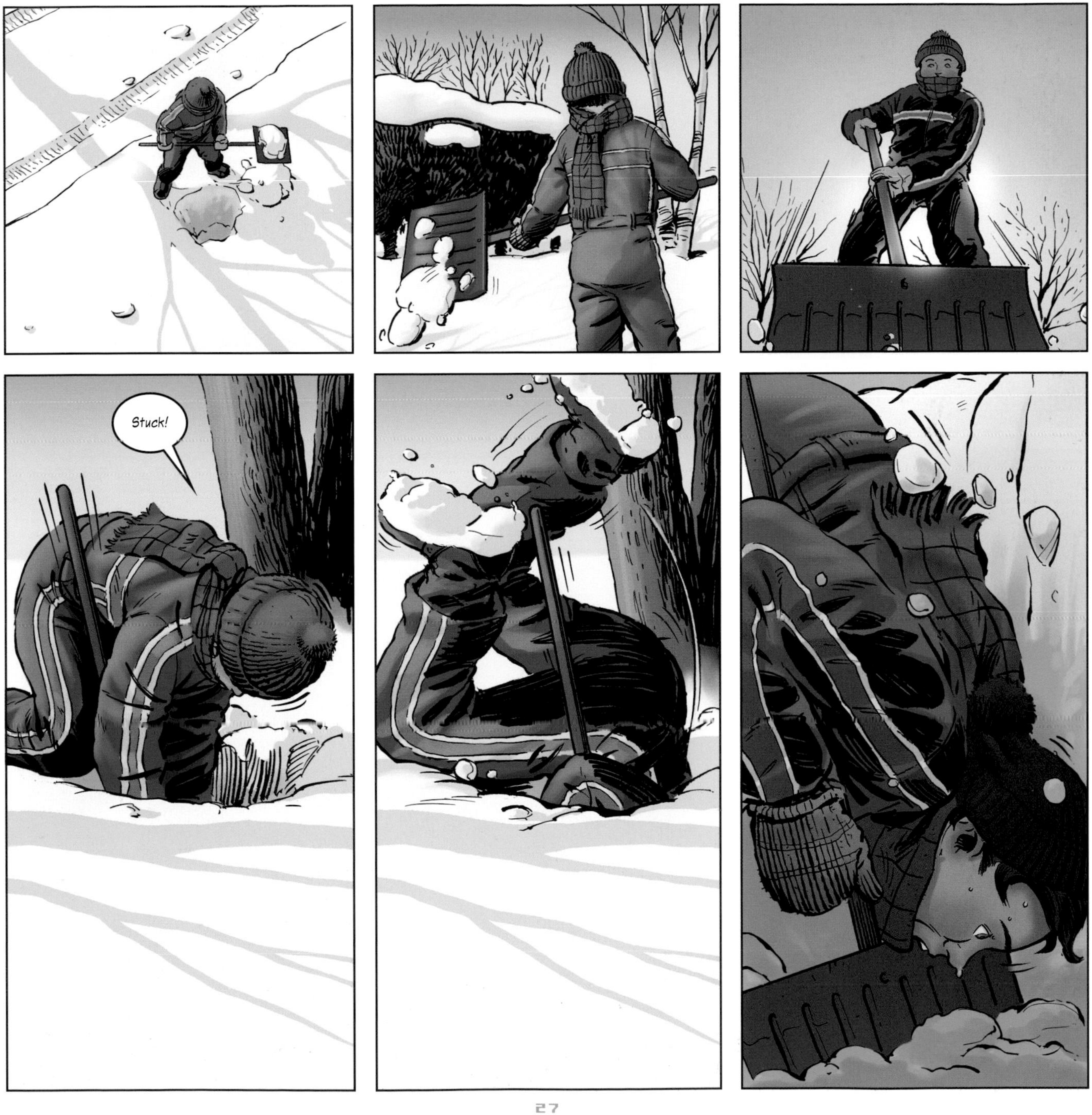
Stuck!

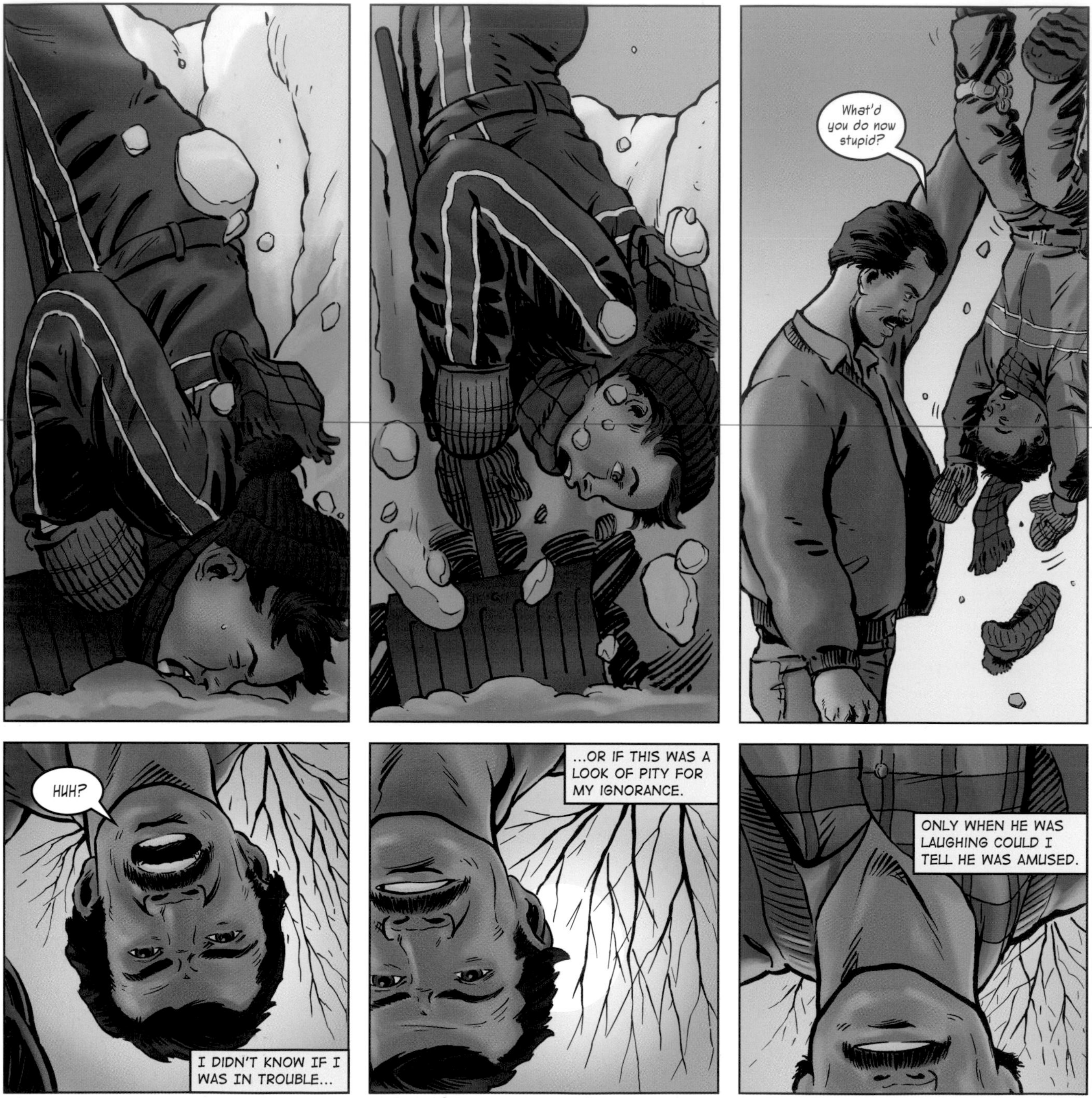
What'd you do now stupid?
HUH?
I DIDN'T KNOW IF I WAS IN TROUBLE...
...OR IF THIS WAS A LOOK OF PITY FOR MY IGNORANCE.
ONLY WHEN HE WAS LAUGHING COULD I TELL HE WAS AMUSED.

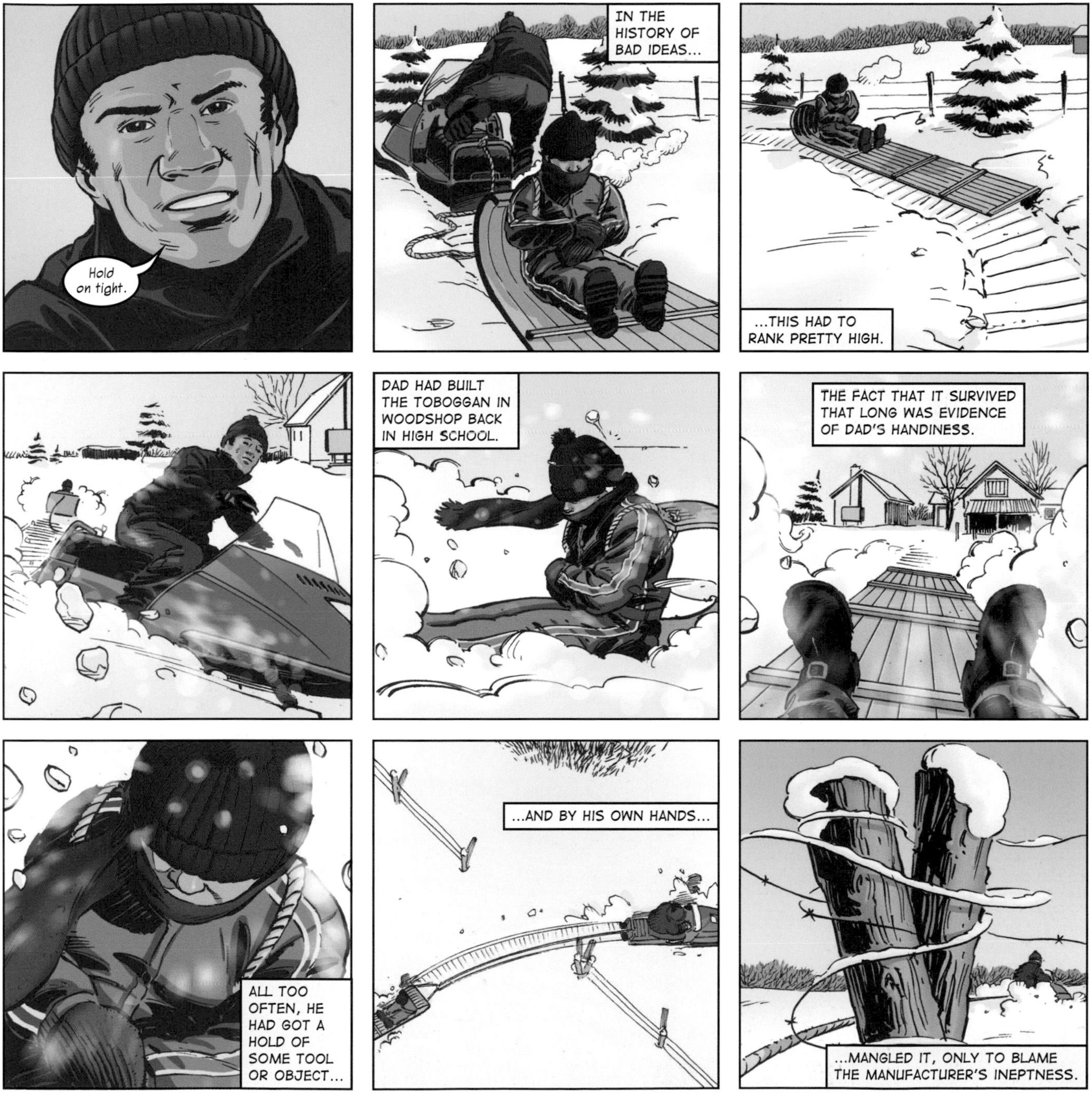
Hold on tight.
IN THE HISTORY OF BAD IDEAS...
...THIS HAD TO RANK PRETTY HIGH.
DAD HAD BUILT THE TOBOGGAN IN WOODSHOP BACK IN HIGH SCHOOL.
THE FACT THAT IT SURVIVED THAT LONG WAS EVIDENCE OF DAD'S HANDINESS.
ALL TOO OFTEN, HE HAD GOT A HOLD OF SOME TOOL OR OBJECT...
...AND BY HIS OWN HANDS...
...MANGLED IT, ONLY TO BLAME THE MANUFACTURER'S INEPTNESS.

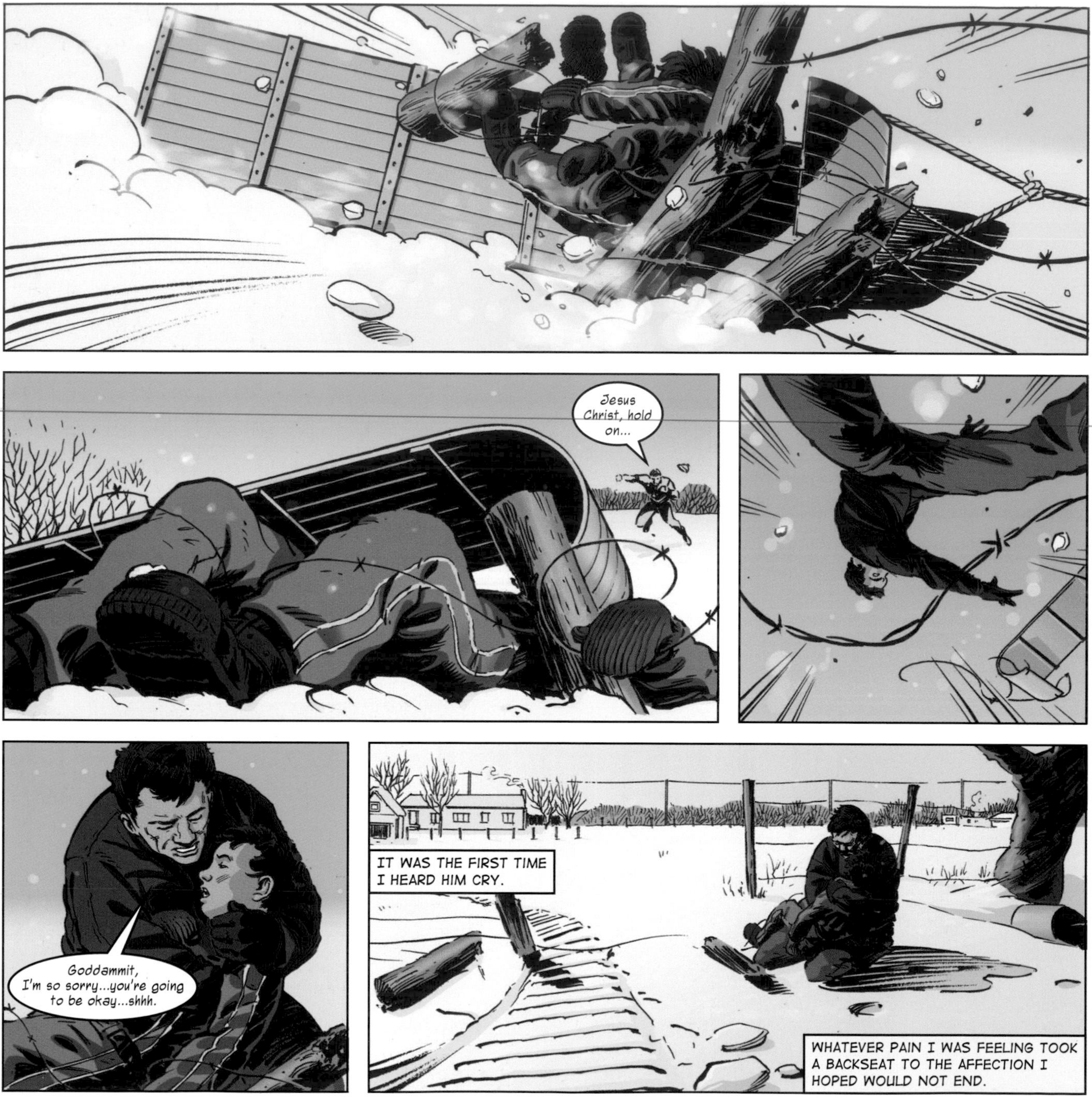

Jesus Christ, hold on...
Goddammit, I'm so sorry...you're going to be okay...shhh.
IT WAS THE FIRST TIME I HEARD HIM CRY.
WHATEVER PAIN I WAS FEELING TOOK A BACKSEAT TO THE AFFECTION I HOPED WOULD NOT END.

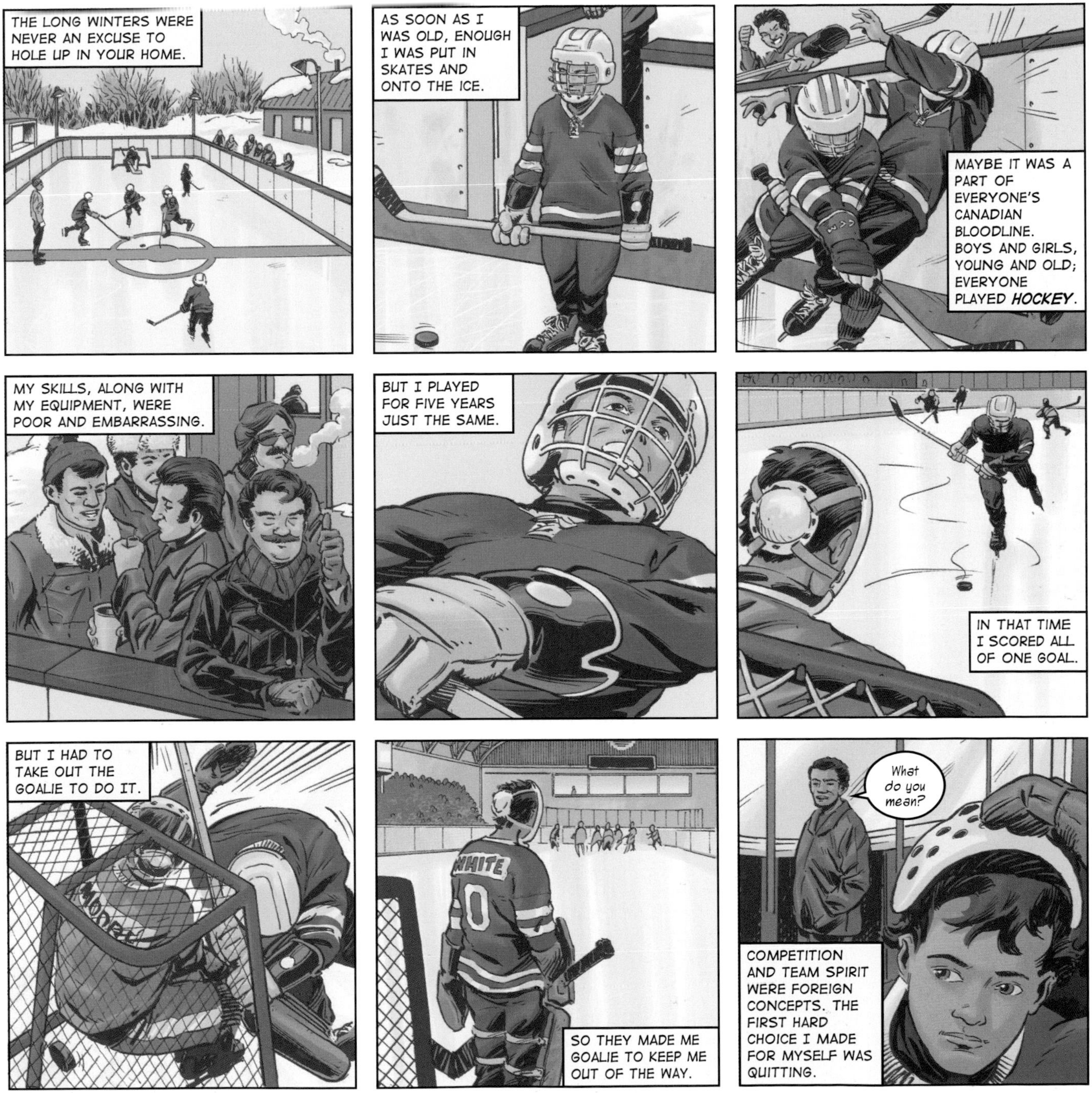
THE LONG WINTERS WERE NEVER AN EXCUSE TO HOLE UP IN YOUR HOME.
AS SOON AS I WAS OLD, ENOUGH I WAS PUT IN SKATES AND ONTO THE ICE.
MAYBE IT WAS A PART OF EVERYONE'S CANADIAN BLOODLINE. BOYS AND GIRLS, YOUNG AND OLD; EVERYONE PLAYED HOCKEY.
MY SKILLS, ALONG WITH MY EQUIPMENT, WERE POOR AND EMBARRASSING.
BUT I PLAYED FOR FIVE YEARS JUST THE SAME.
IN THAT TIME I SCORED ALL OF ONE GOAL.
BUT I HAD TO TAKE OUT THE GOALIE TO DO IT.
WHITE
0
SO THEY MADE ME GOALIE TO KEEP ME OUT OF THE WAY.
What do you mean?
COMPETITION AND TEAM SPIRIT WERE FOREIGN CONCEPTS. THE FIRST HARD CHOICE I MADE FOR MYSELF WAS QUITTING.

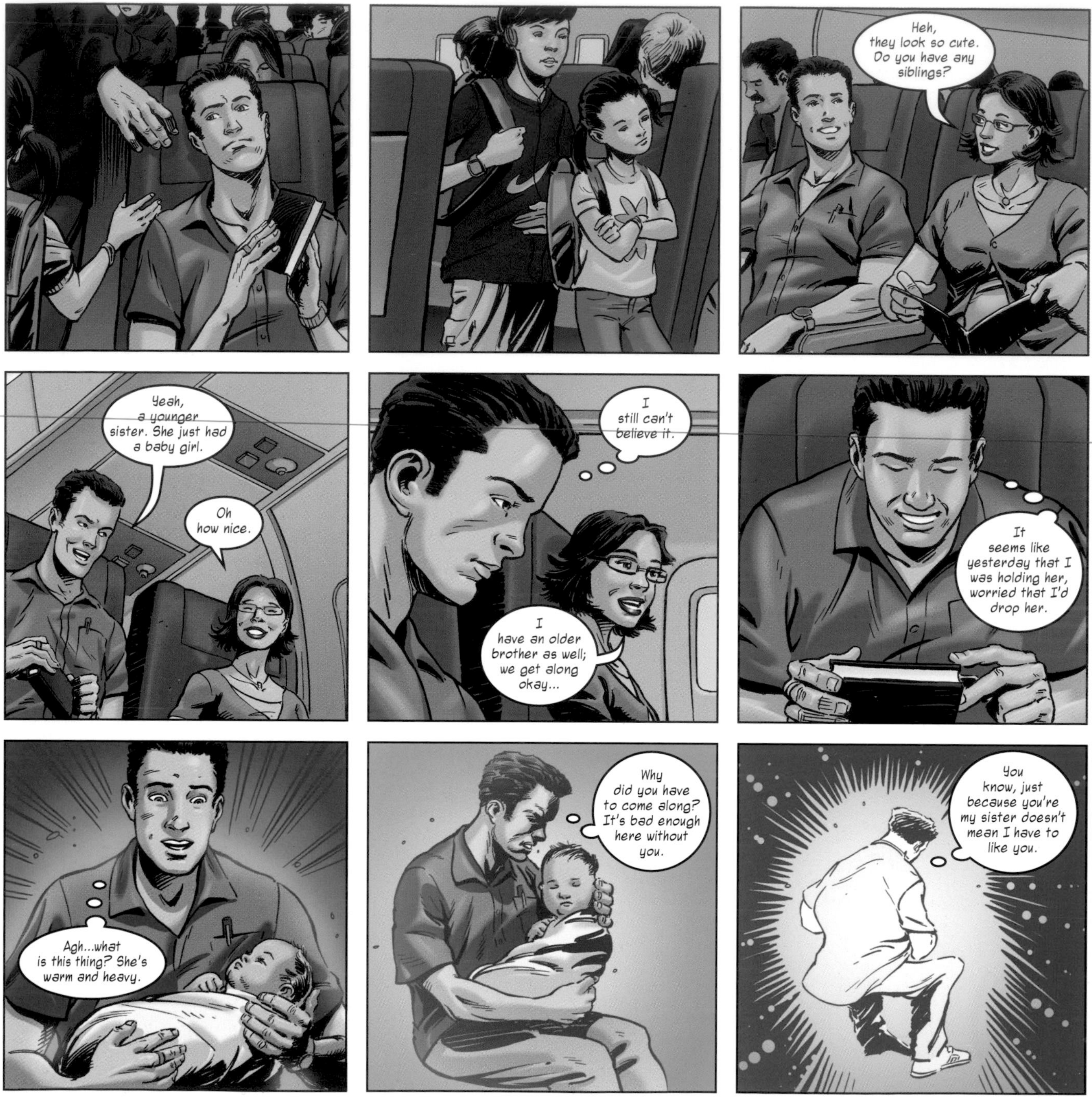

Heh, they look so cute. Do you have any siblings?
Yeah, a younger sister. She just had a baby girl.
Oh how nice.
I still can't believe it.
I have an older brother as well; we get along okay...
It seems like yesterday that I was holding her, worried that I'd drop her.
Agh...what is this thing? She's warm and heavy.
Why did you have to come along? It's bad enough here without you.
You know, just because you're my sister doesn't mean I have to like you.

...he lives with his family in Iowa, but we don't talk much.

Yeah, it can be tough sometimes.

Heck, it took me 15 years just to become friends with my sister.

Guess I had too much emotional baggage.

Please prepare the cabin for take-off.

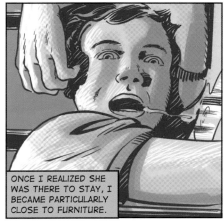

ONCE I REALIZED SHE WAS THERE TO STAY, I BECAME PARTICULARLY CLOSE TO FURNITURE.

I'M NOT SURE IT WAS THE FURNITURE STYLES PER SE, AS MUCH AS THEIR INERTNESS.

MOSTLY, I PRETENDED THAT I WAS DEAD. DEAD AND MISSING.

IT WAS COMFORTING KNOWING THAT MOM AND DAD'S ATTENTION WAS ELSEWHERE. IT ACTUALLY GAVE ME SOME ROOM TO BREATHE.

AT SOME POINT THOUGH, I COULDN'T TAKE IT ANYMORE. I FELT IGNORED, SOMETHING I WOULD COME TO HATE.

I'D DO WHAT I COULD TO GET THEM TO LOOK FOR ME.

Shane! Now where'd he go off to so early?

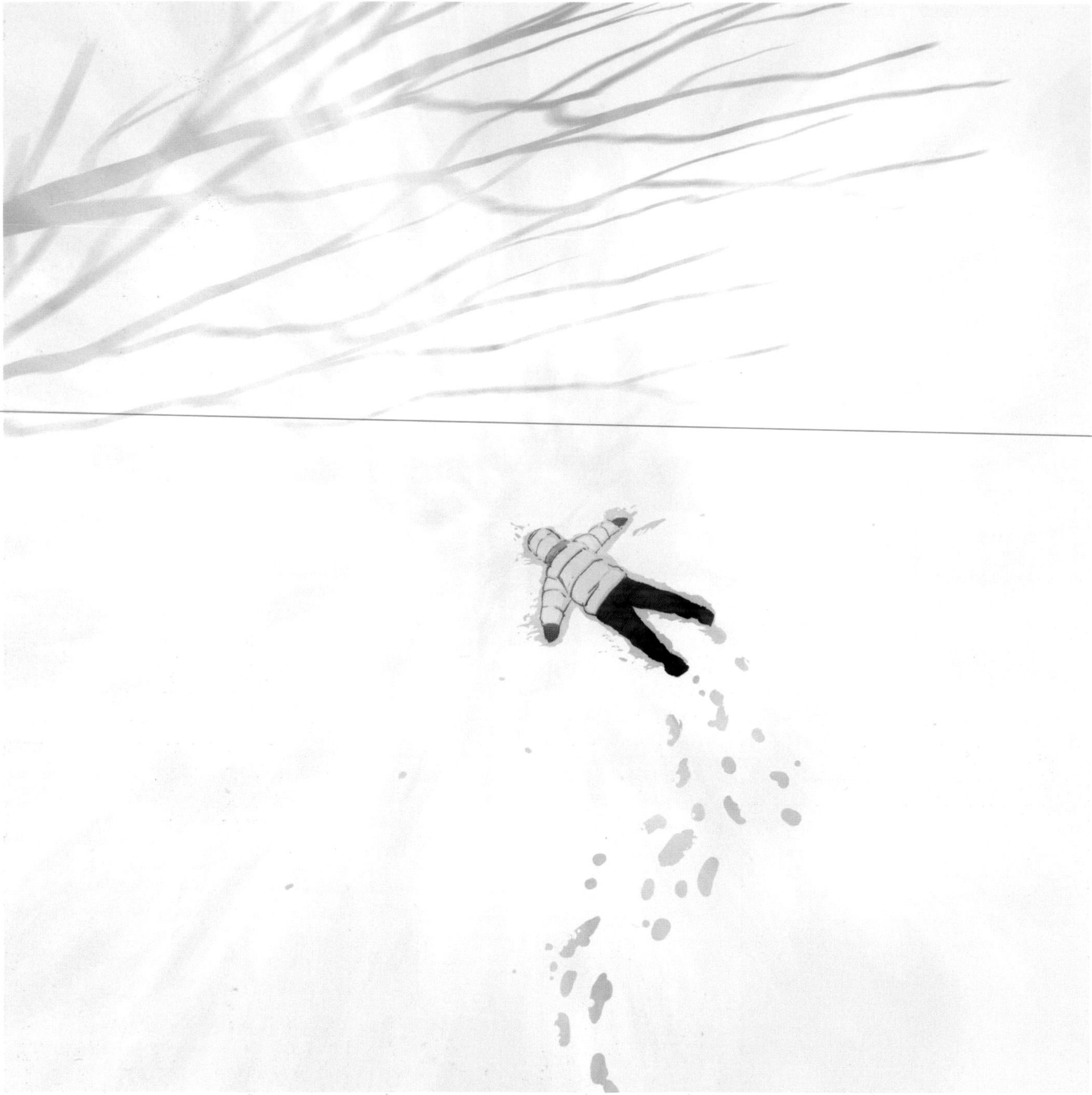

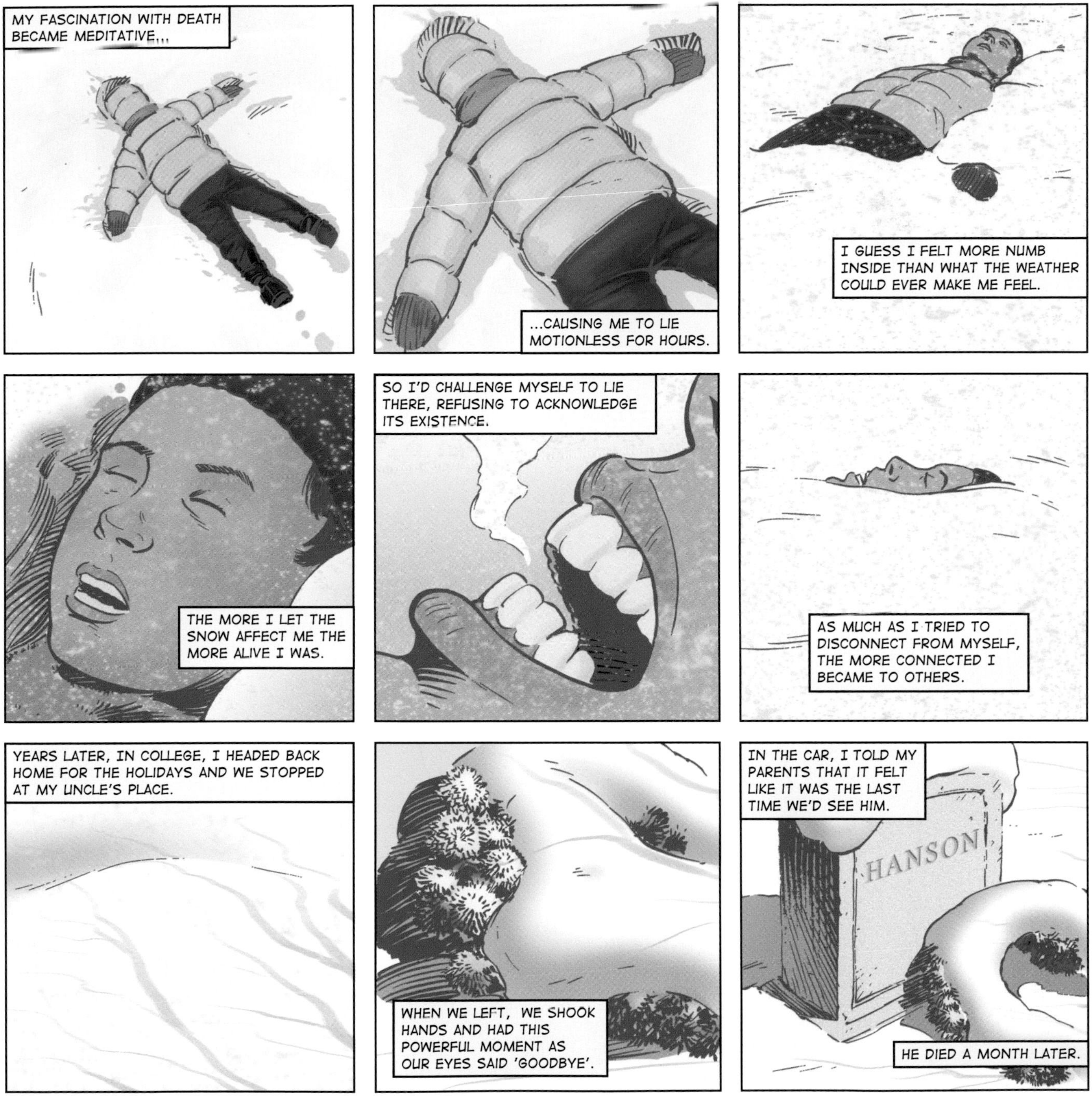
MY FASCINATION WITH DEATH BECAME MEDITATIVE...
...CAUSING ME TO LIE MOTIONLESS FOR HOURS.
I GUESS I FELT MORE NUMB INSIDE THAN WHAT THE WEATHER COULD EVER MAKE ME FEEL.
THE MORE I LET THE SNOW AFFECT ME THE MORE ALIVE I WAS.
SO I'D CHALLENGE MYSELF TO LIE THERE, REFUSING TO ACKNOWLEDGE ITS EXISTENCE.
AS MUCH AS I TRIED TO DISCONNECT FROM MYSELF, THE MORE CONNECTED I BECAME TO OTHERS.
YEARS LATER, IN COLLEGE, I HEADED BACK HOME FOR THE HOLIDAYS AND WE STOPPED AT MY UNCLE'S PLACE.
WHEN WE LEFT, WE SHOOK HANDS AND HAD THIS POWERFUL MOMENT AS OUR EYES SAID 'GOODBYE'.
IN THE CAR, I TOLD MY PARENTS THAT IT FELT LIKE IT WAS THE LAST TIME WE'D SEE HIM.
HANSON
HE DIED A MONTH LATER.

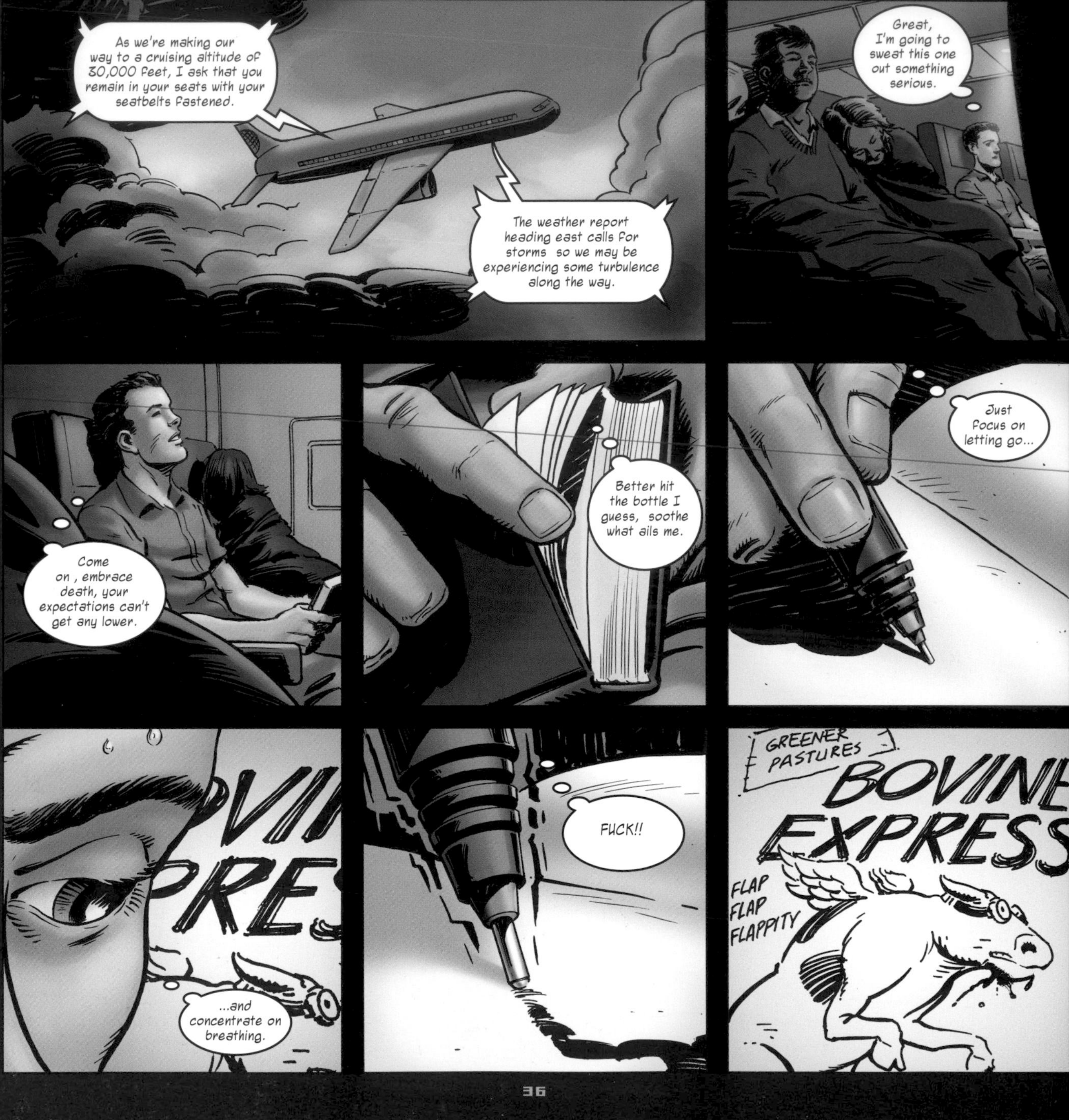

As we're making our way to a cruising altitude of 30,000 feet, I ask that you remain in your seats with your seatbelts fastened.
The weather report heading east calls for storms so we may be experiencing some turbulence along the way.
Great, I'm going to sweat this one out something serious.
Come on , embrace death, your expectations can't get any lower.
Better hit the bottle I guess, soothe what ails me.
Just focus on letting go...
...and concentrate on breathing.
FUCK!!
GREENER PASTURES
BOVINE EXPRESS
FLAP
FLAP
FLAPPITY

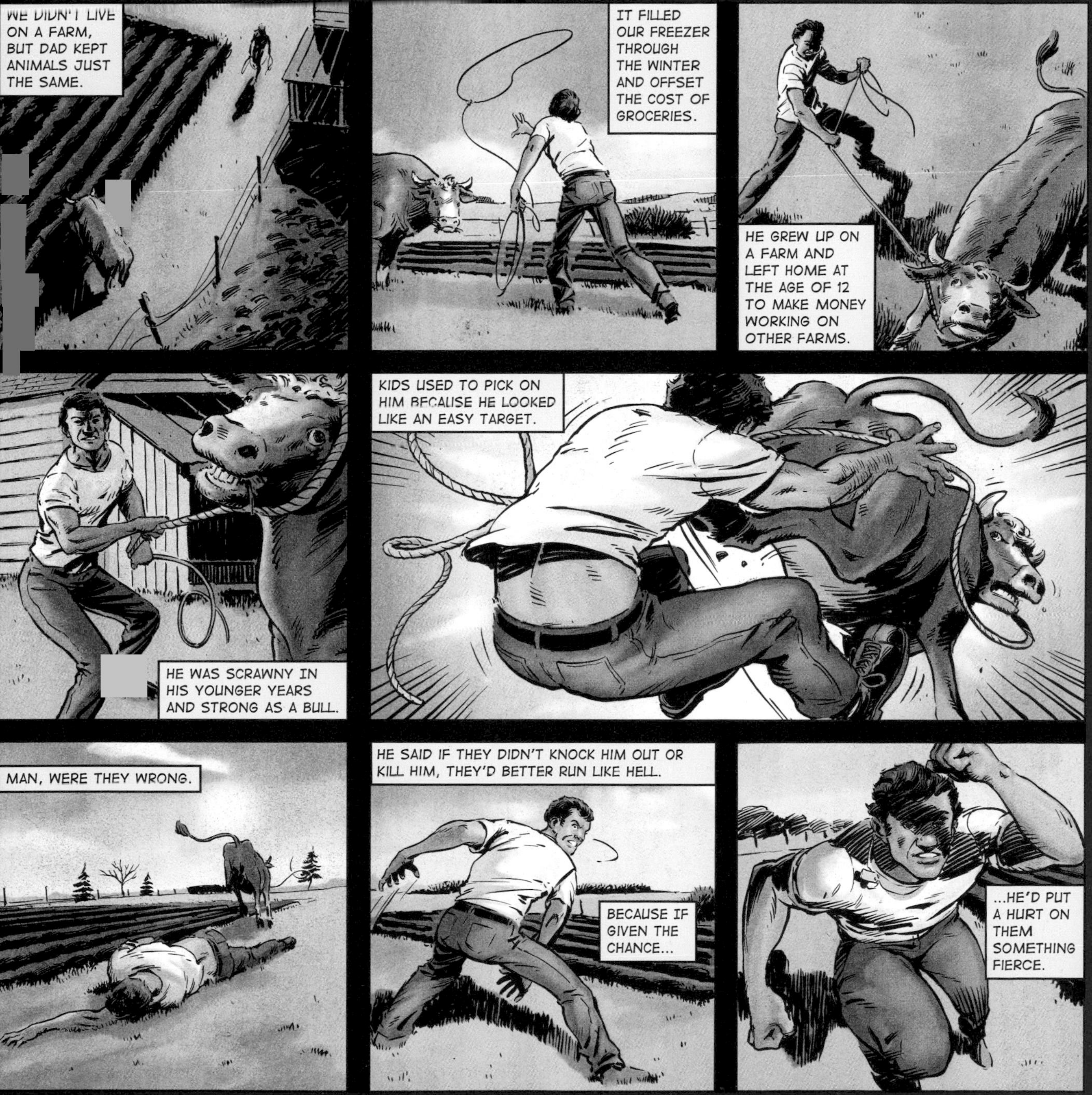
WE DIDN'T LIVE ON A FARM, BUT DAD KEPT ANIMALS JUST THE SAME.
IT FILLED OUR FREEZER THROUGH THE WINTER AND OFFSET THE COST OF GROCERIES.
HE GREW UP ON A FARM AND LEFT HOME AT THE AGE OF 12 TO MAKE MONEY WORKING ON OTHER FARMS.
HE WAS SCRAWNY IN HIS YOUNGER YEARS AND STRONG AS A BULL.
KIDS USED TO PICK ON HIM BECAUSE HE LOOKED LIKE AN EASY TARGET.
MAN, WERE THEY WRONG.
HE SAID IF THEY DIDN'T KNOCK HIM OUT OR KILL HIM, THEY'D BETTER RUN LIKE HELL.
BECAUSE IF GIVEN THE CHANCE...
...HE'D PUT A HURT ON THEM SOMETHING FIERCE.

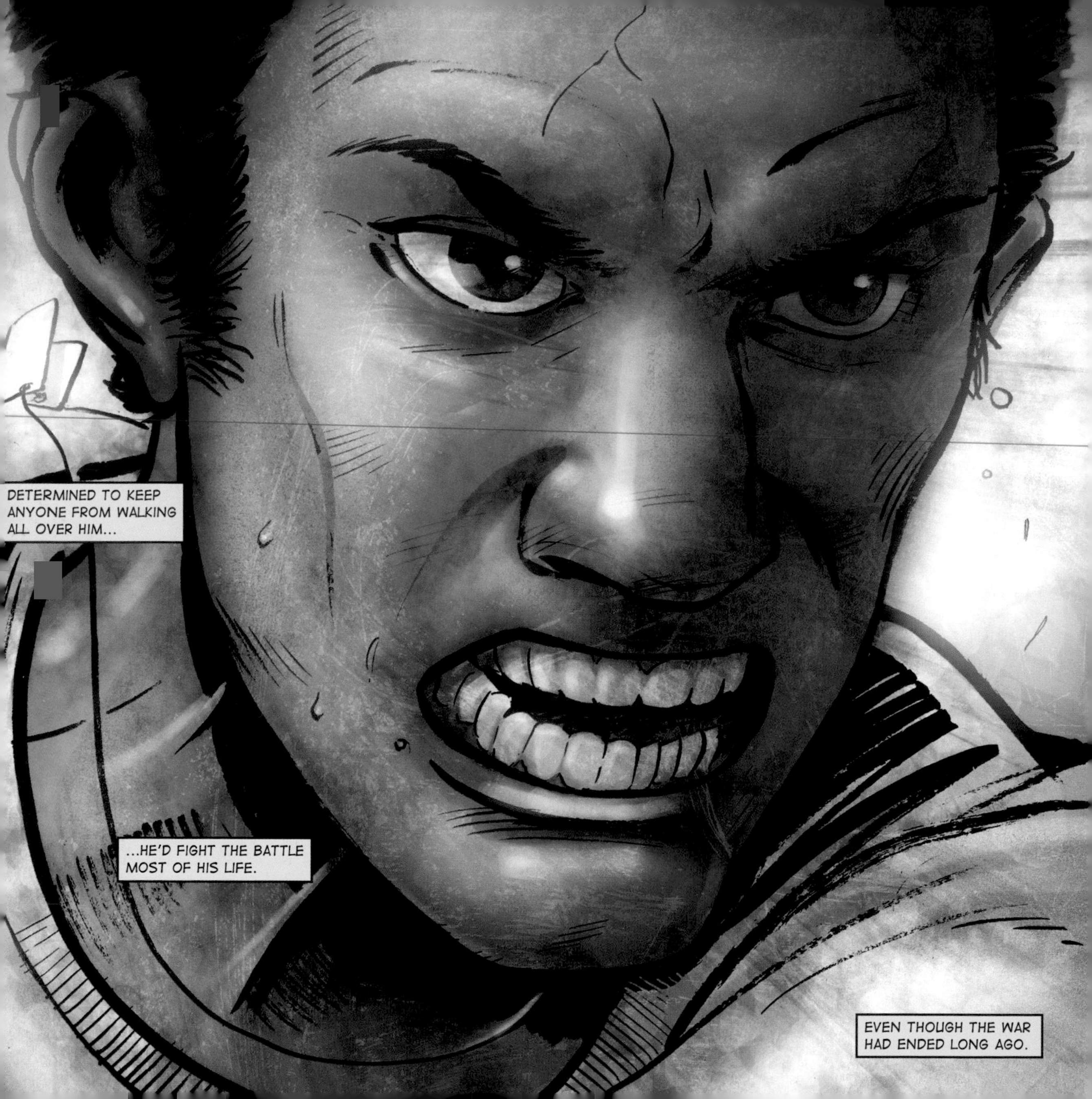
DETERMINED TO KEEP ANYONE FROM WALKING ALL OVER HIM...
...HE'D FIGHT THE BATTLE MOST OF HIS LIFE.
EVEN THOUGH THE WAR HAD ENDED LONG AGO.

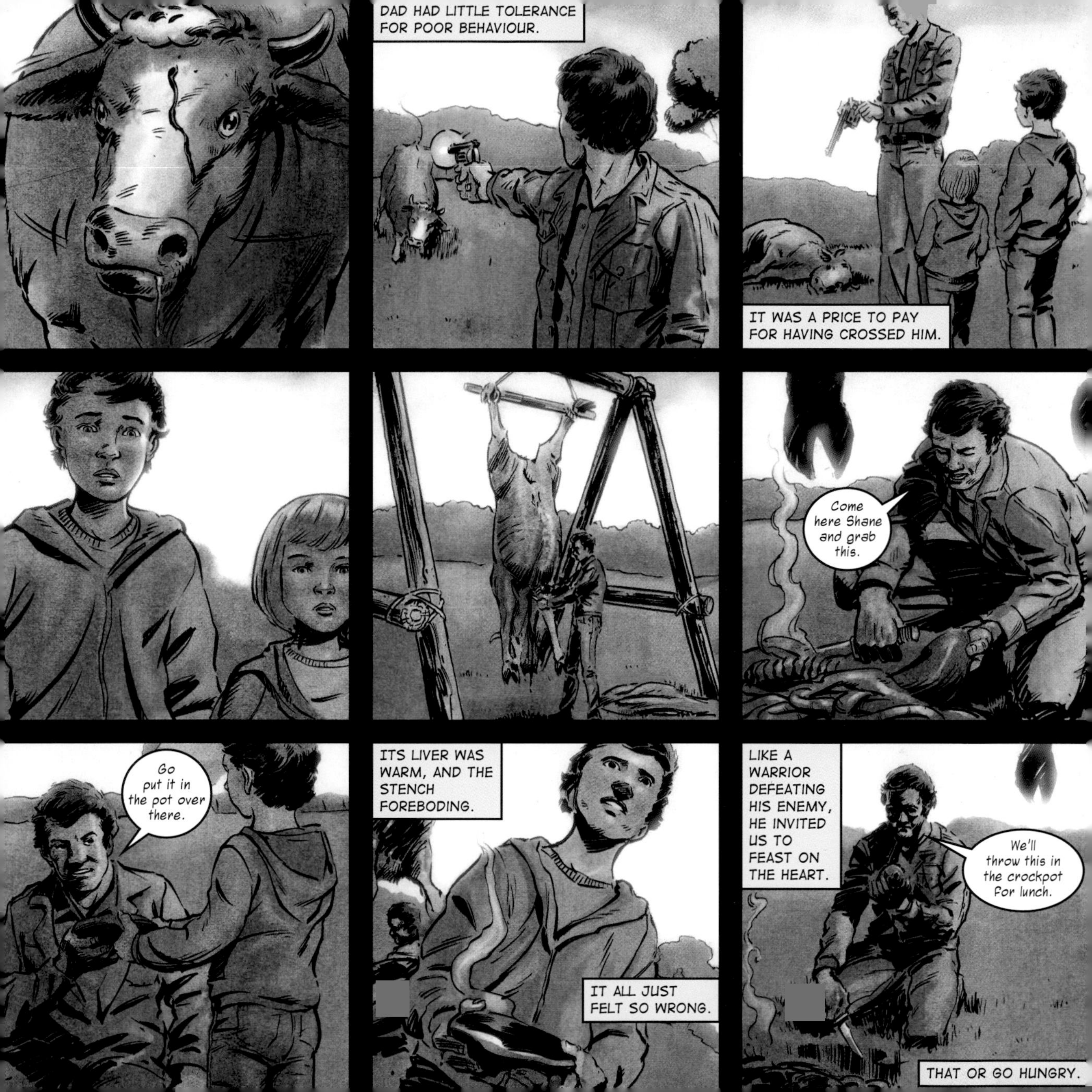
DAD HAD LITTLE TOLERANCE FOR POOR BEHAVIOUR.
IT WAS A PRICE TO PAY FOR HAVING CROSSED HIM.
Come here Shane and grab this.
Go put it in the pot over there.
ITS LIVER WAS WARM, AND THE STENCH FOREBODING.
IT ALL JUST FELT SO WRONG.
LIKE A WARRIOR DEFEATING HIS ENEMY, HE INVITED US TO FEAST ON THE HEART.
We'll throw this in the crockpot for lunch.
THAT OR GO HUNGRY.

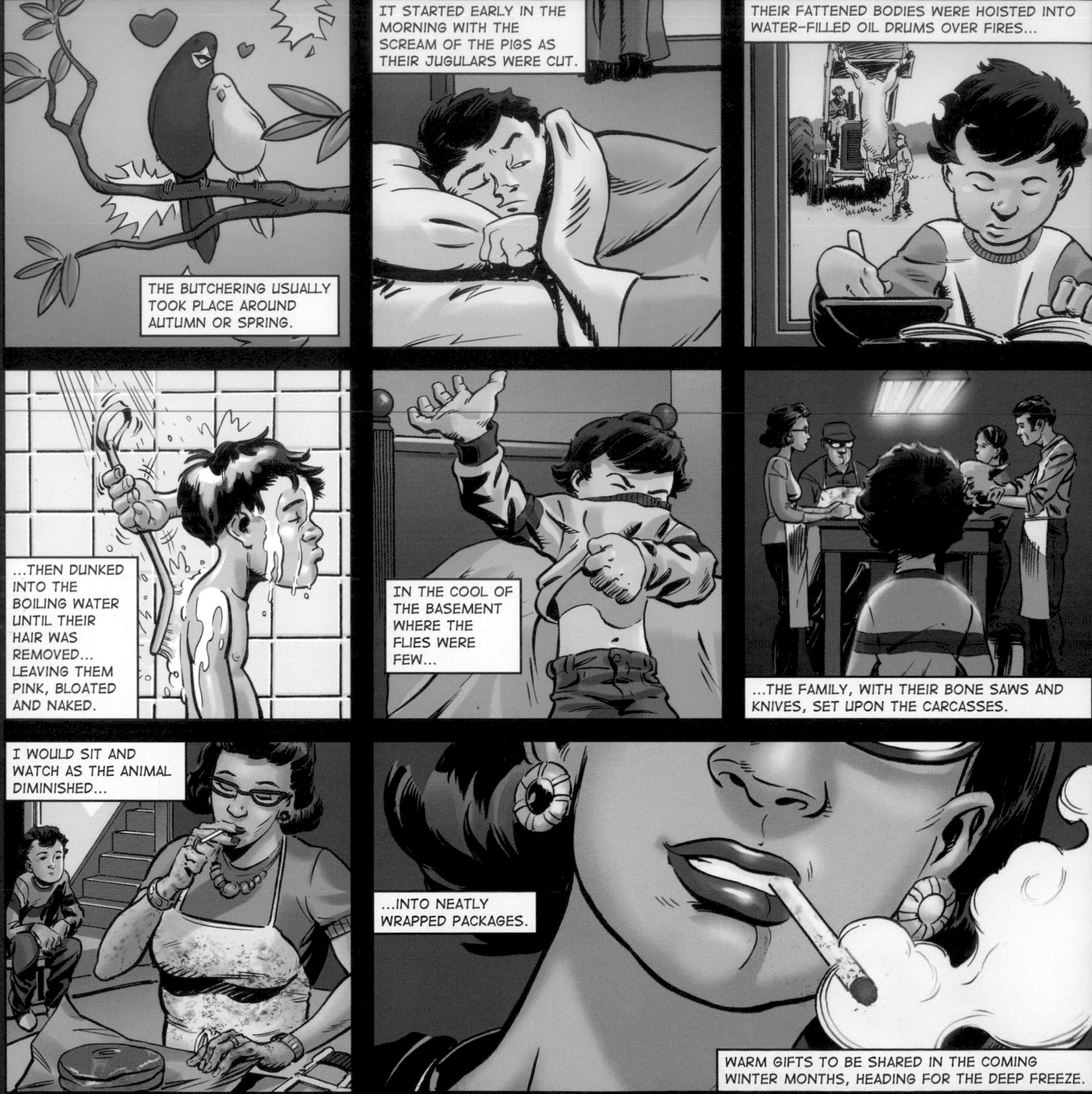
THE BUTCHERING USUALLY TOOK PLACE AROUND AUTUMN OR SPRING.
IT STARTED EARLY IN THE MORNING WITH THE SCREAM OF THE PIGS AS THEIR JUGULARS WERE CUT.
THEIR FATTENED BODIES WERE HOISTED INTO WATER-FILLED OIL DRUMS OVER FIRES...
...THEN DUNKED INTO THE BOILING WATER UNTIL THEIR HAIR WAS REMOVED... LEAVING THEM PINK, BLOATED AND NAKED.
IN THE COOL OF THE BASEMENT WHERE THE FLIES WERE FEW...
...THE FAMILY, WITH THEIR BONE SAWS AND KNIVES, SET UPON THE CARCASSES.
I WOULD SIT AND WATCH AS THE ANIMAL DIMINISHED...
...INTO NEATLY WRAPPED PACKAGES.
WARM GIFTS TO BE SHARED IN THE COMING WINTER MONTHS, HEADING FOR THE DEEP FREEZE.

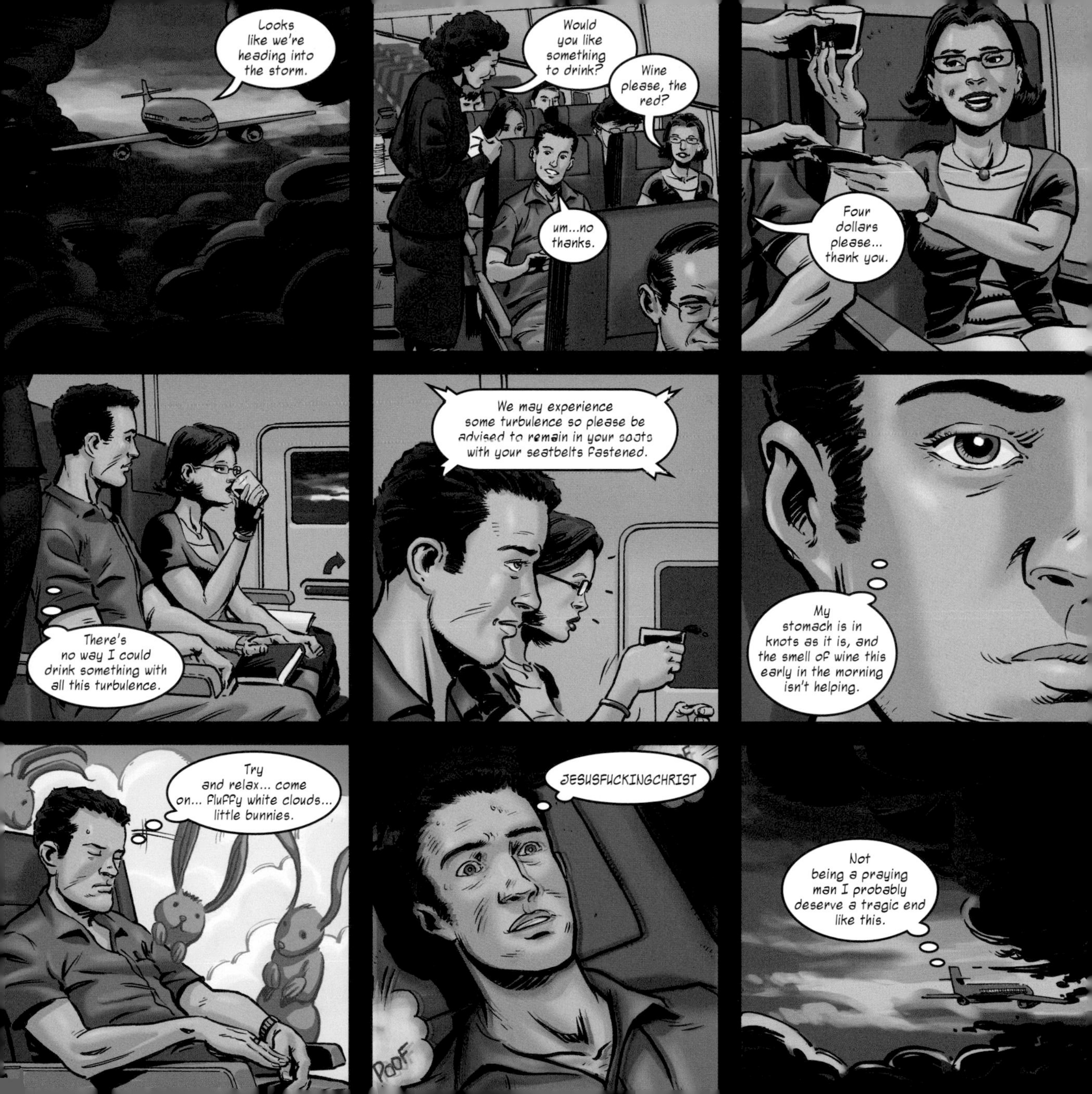

Looks like we're heading into the storm.
Would you like something to drink?
Wine please, the red?
um...no thanks.
Four dollars please... thank you.
There's no way I could drink something with all this turbulence.
We may experience some turbulence so please be advised to remain in your seats with your seatbelts fastened.
My stomach is in knots as it is, and the smell of wine this early in the morning isn't helping.
Try and relax... come on... fluffy white clouds... little bunnies.
JESUSFUCKINGCHRIST
POOF
Not being a praying man I probably deserve a tragic end like this.

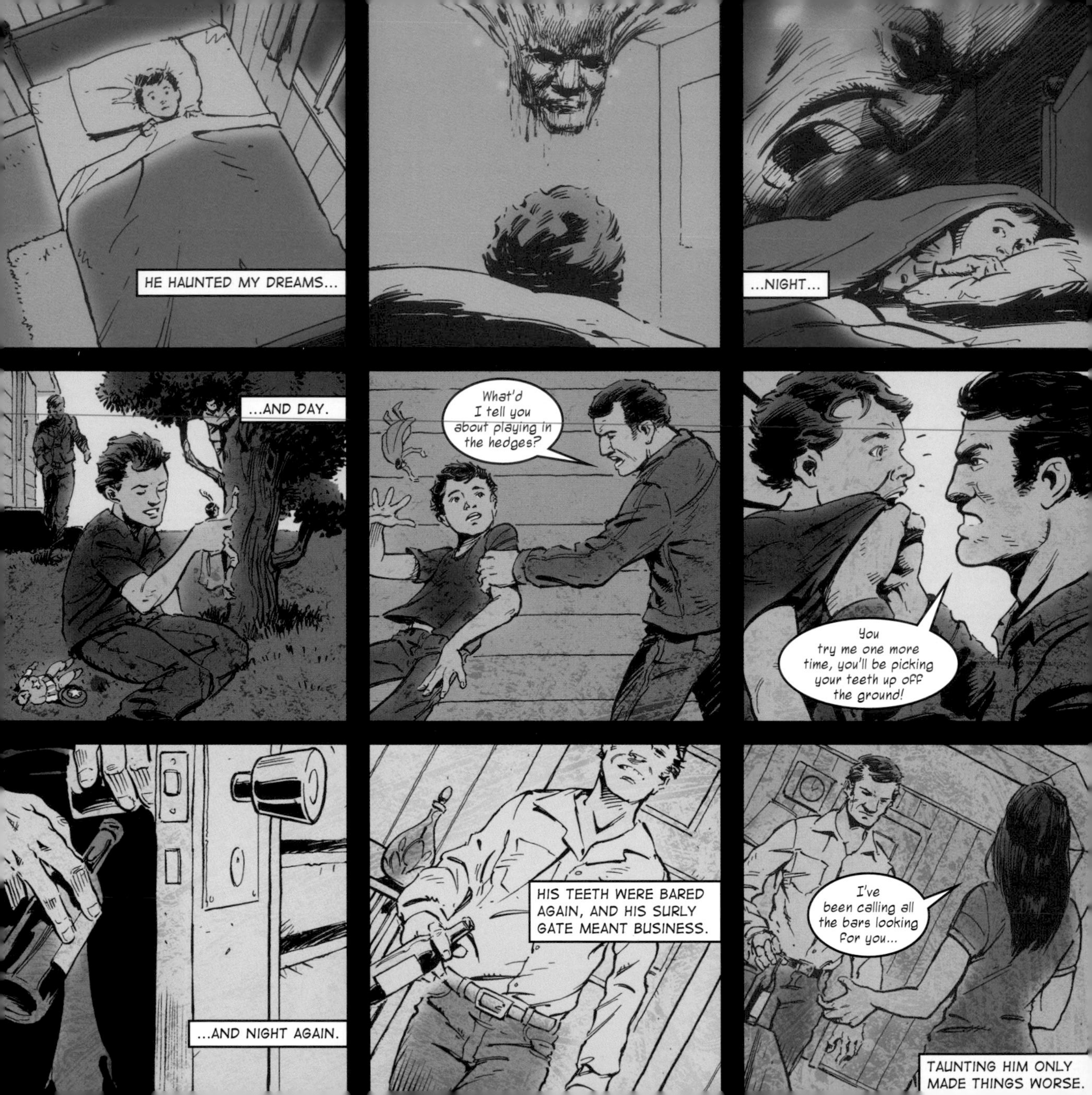
HE HAUNTED MY DREAMS...
...NIGHT...
...AND DAY.
What'd I tell you about playing in the hedges?
You try me one more time, you'll be picking your teeth up off the ground!
...AND NIGHT AGAIN.
HIS TEETH WERE BARED AGAIN, AND HIS SURLY GATE MEANT BUSINESS.
I've been calling all the bars looking for you...
TAUNTING HIM ONLY MADE THINGS WORSE.

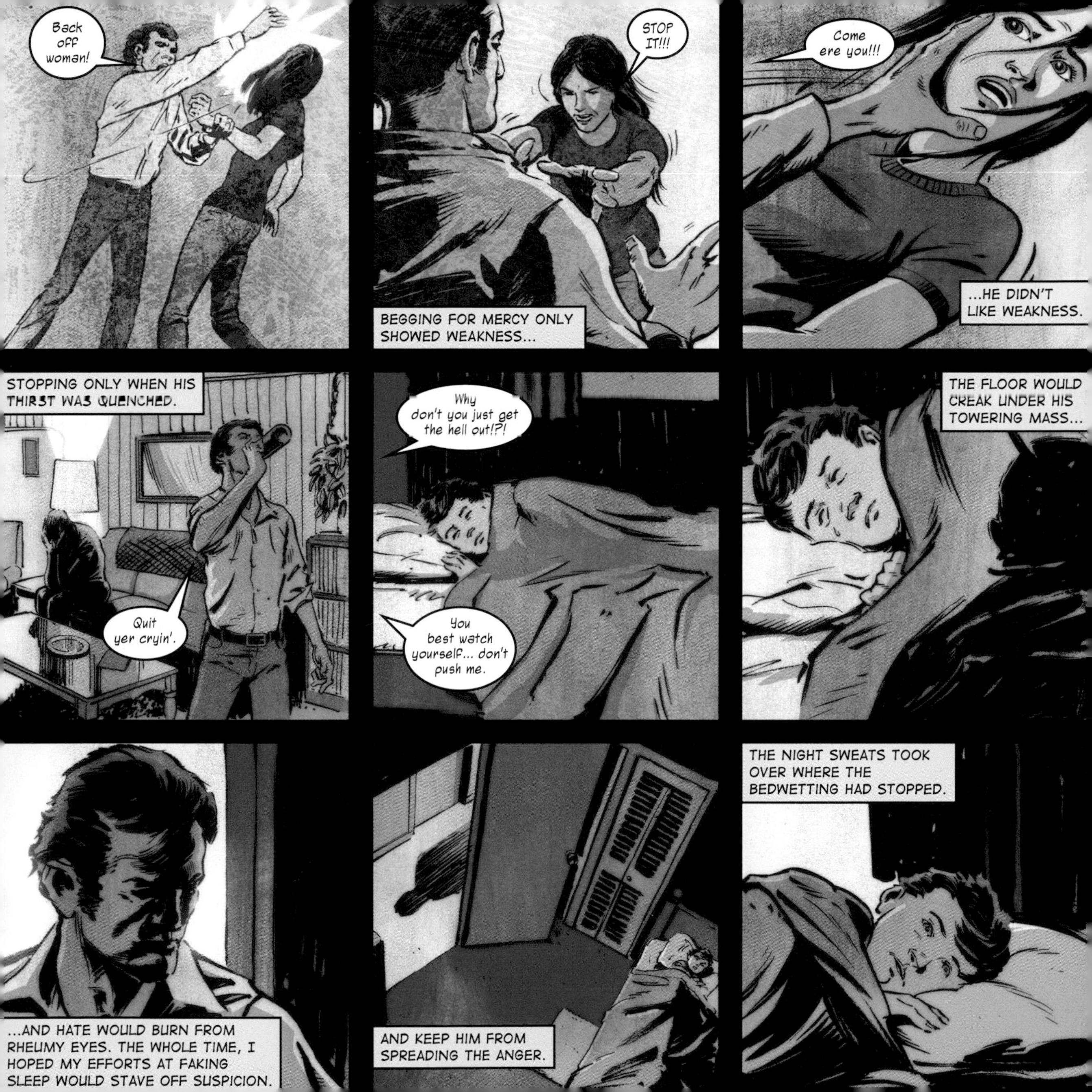

Back off woman!
STOP IT!!!
BEGGING FOR MERCY ONLY SHOWED WEAKNESS...
Come ere you!!!
...HE DIDN'T LIKE WEAKNESS.
STOPPING ONLY WHEN HIS THIRST WAS QUENCHED.
Quit yer cryin'.
Why don't you just get the hell out!?!
You best watch yourself... don't push me.
THE FLOOR WOULD CREAK UNDER HIS TOWERING MASS...
...AND HATE WOULD BURN FROM RHEUMY EYES. THE WHOLE TIME, I HOPED MY EFFORTS AT FAKING SLEEP WOULD STAVE OFF SUSPICION.
AND KEEP HIM FROM SPREADING THE ANGER.
THE NIGHT SWEATS TOOK OVER WHERE THE BEDWETTING HAD STOPPED.

FALLING ASLEEP WAS LABORIOUS.

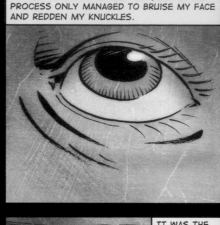

I TRIED TO KNOCK MYSELF OUT, BUT IN THE PROCESS ONLY MANAGED TO BRUISE MY FACE AND REDDEN MY KNUCKLES.

AT ONE POINT I EMBRACED SATAN.

I TRADED MY SOUL FOR A CHANCE TO SURVIVE THE RULING FIST OF A DRUNKEN GOD.

IT WAS THE ONLY FIGHT I COULD GIVE.

ANY DIRECT CONFRONTATION WOULD HAVE MEANT CERTAIN DEATH, WHICH I BELIEVED FOR YEARS..

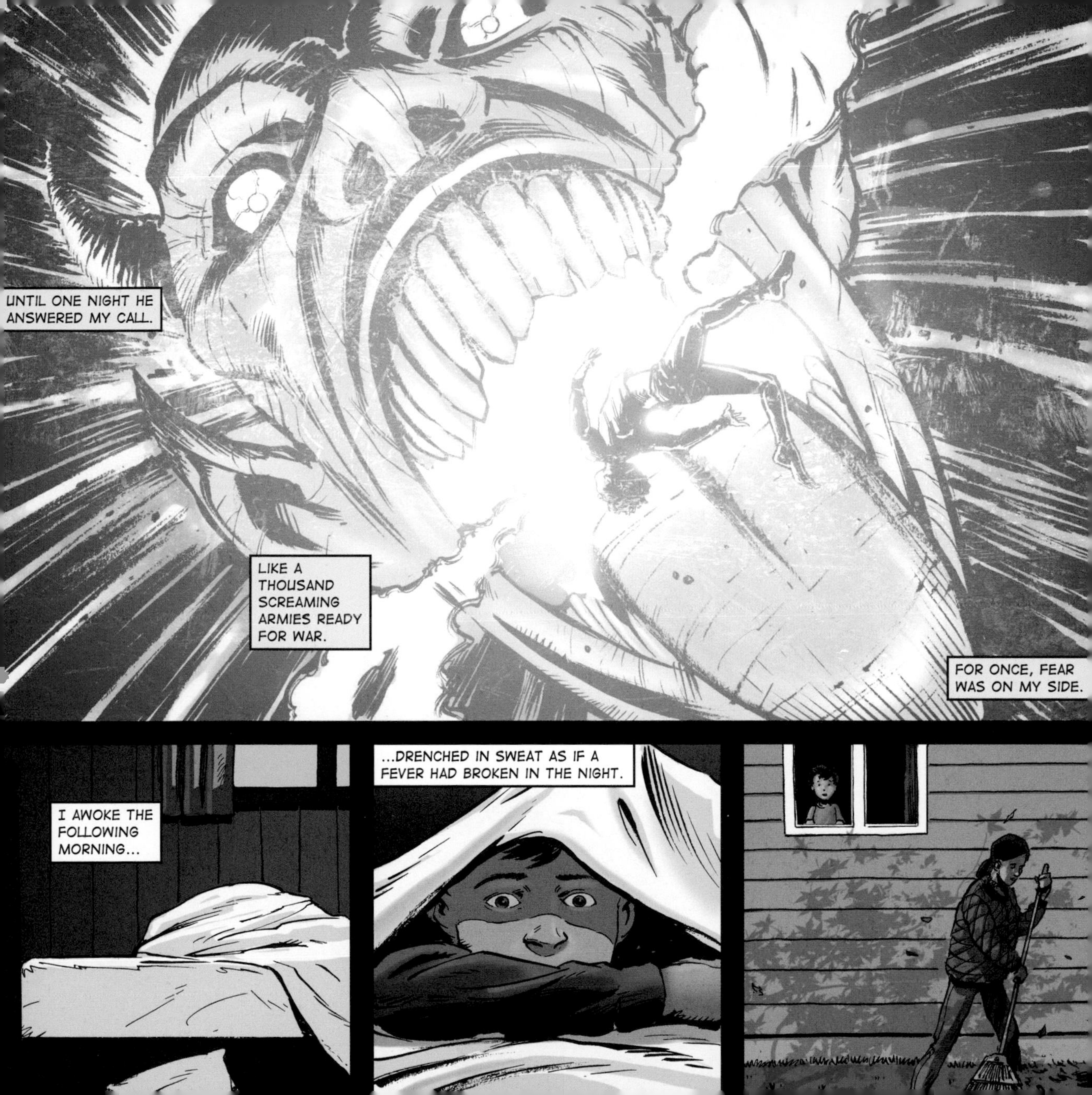
UNTIL ONE NIGHT HE ANSWERED MY CALL.
LIKE A THOUSAND SCREAMING ARMIES READY FOR WAR.
FOR ONCE, FEAR WAS ON MY SIDE.
I AWOKE THE FOLLOWING MORNING...
...DRENCHED IN SWEAT AS IF A FEVER HAD BROKEN IN THE NIGHT.

I READILY ADMIT, I WASN'T SURE IF MY LIFE HAD CHANGED AFTER THAT NIGHT.

Would it hurt just once to take a break from work to do something I want to do?

Like what, spend money all day on stupid shit?

THE NERVOUS SWEAT THAT CAME WITH THE HEATED TALK AT DINNER CERTAINLY FELT THE SAME.

THEN I NOTICED THE KETCHUP ON MY SISTER'S FACE.

UNTHINKINGLY, I STARTED TO LAUGH.

BAD MOVE.

How'd you like to laugh outta the other side of your face?

I'm not laughing at you...

I was just...

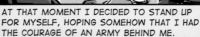

AT THAT MOMENT I DECIDED TO STAND UP FOR MYSELF, HOPING SOMEHOW THAT I HAD THE COURAGE OF AN ARMY BEHIND ME.

You know what your problem is?

BUT HE WAS TOO DRUNK TO RECOGNIZE ANYONE ELSE'S GOD...

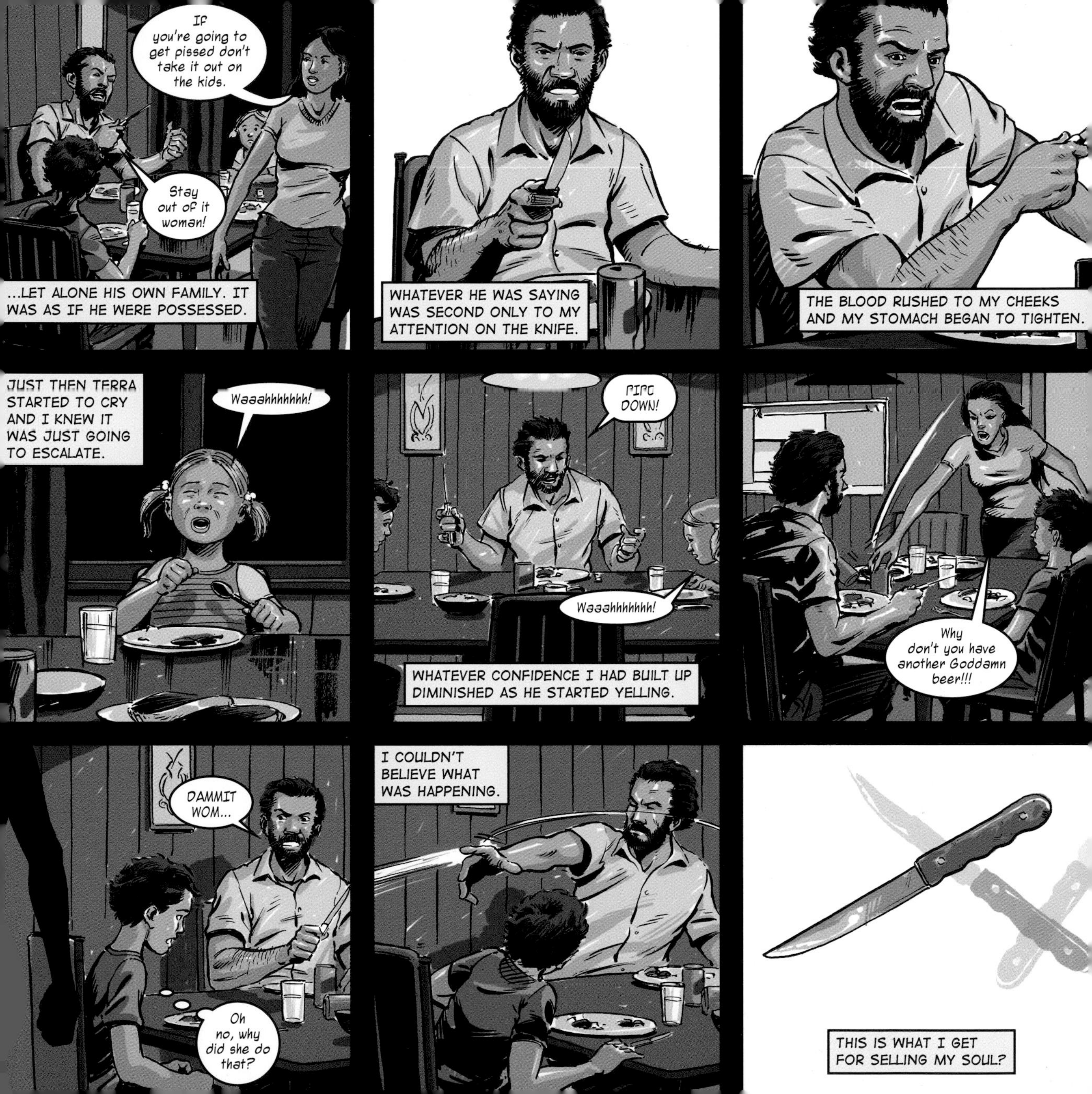
If you're going to get pissed don't take it out on the kids.
Stay out of it woman!
...LET ALONE HIS OWN FAMILY. IT WAS AS IF HE WERE POSSESSED.
WHATEVER HE WAS SAYING WAS SECOND ONLY TO MY ATTENTION ON THE KNIFE.
THE BLOOD RUSHED TO MY CHEEKS AND MY STOMACH BEGAN TO TIGHTEN.
JUST THEN TERRA STARTED TO CRY AND I KNEW IT WAS JUST GOING TO ESCALATE.
Waaahhhhhhh!
PIPE DOWN!
Waaahhhhhhh!
WHATEVER CONFIDENCE I HAD BUILT UP DIMINISHED AS HE STARTED YELLING.
Why don't you have another Goddamn beer!!!
DAMMIT WOM...
Oh no, why did she do that?
I COULDN'T BELIEVE WHAT WAS HAPPENING.
THIS IS WHAT I GET FOR SELLING MY SOUL?

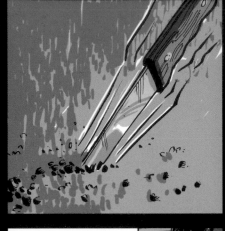

I WAS SURE SHE WAS DEAD.

INCESSANTLY IT LASTED ANOTHER TWENTY MINUTES...

MAYBE IT WAS PAYBACK FOR THE TIME MOM THREW BOILING COFFEE AT HIM.

...BEFORE DAD LEFT TO SOBER UP OR GET DRUNKER.

HE WAS HURT TO THE POINT WHERE HE HAD TO DRAIN THE BLISTERS ON HIS ARM.

ONE DAY WHEN HE WAS CHANGING HIS GAUZE THE LIQUID HAD SQUIRTED ME IN THE FACE.

I LAUGHED BECAUSE IT TICKLED, I DIDN'T KNOW ANY BETTER.

HE'D SAID "YOU THINK THAT'S FUNNY?"

AGAIN, I CRIED.

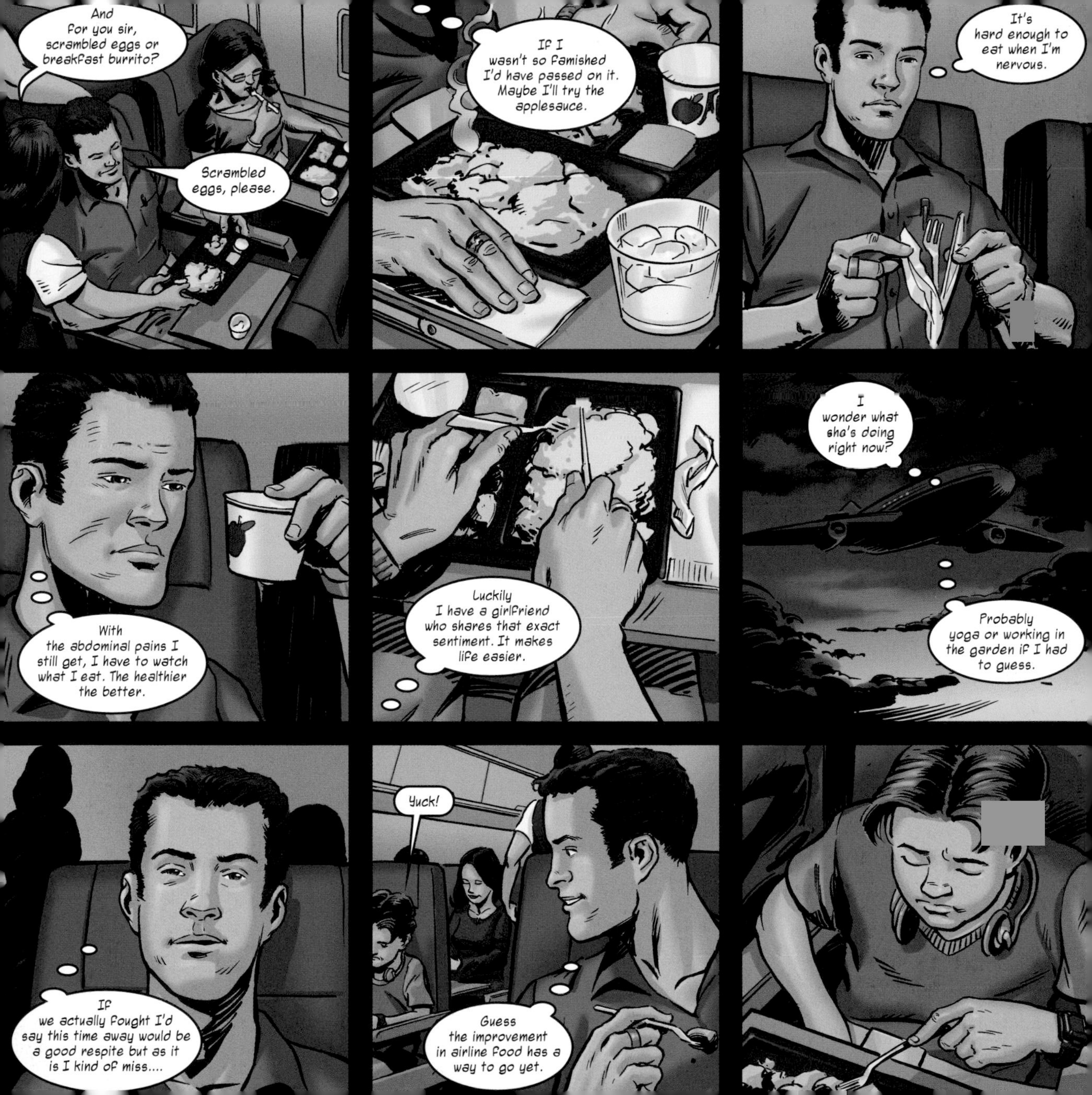
And for you sir, scrambled eggs or breakfast burrito?
Scrambled eggs, please.
If I wasn't so famished I'd have passed on it. Maybe I'll try the applesauce.
It's hard enough to eat when I'm nervous.
With the abdominal pains I still get, I have to watch what I eat. The healthier the better.
Luckily I have a girlfriend who shares that exact sentiment. It makes life easier.
I wonder what she's doing right now?
Probably yoga or working in the garden if I had to guess.
If we actually fought I'd say this time away would be a good respite but as it is I kind of miss....
Yuck!
Guess the improvement in airline food has a way to go yet.

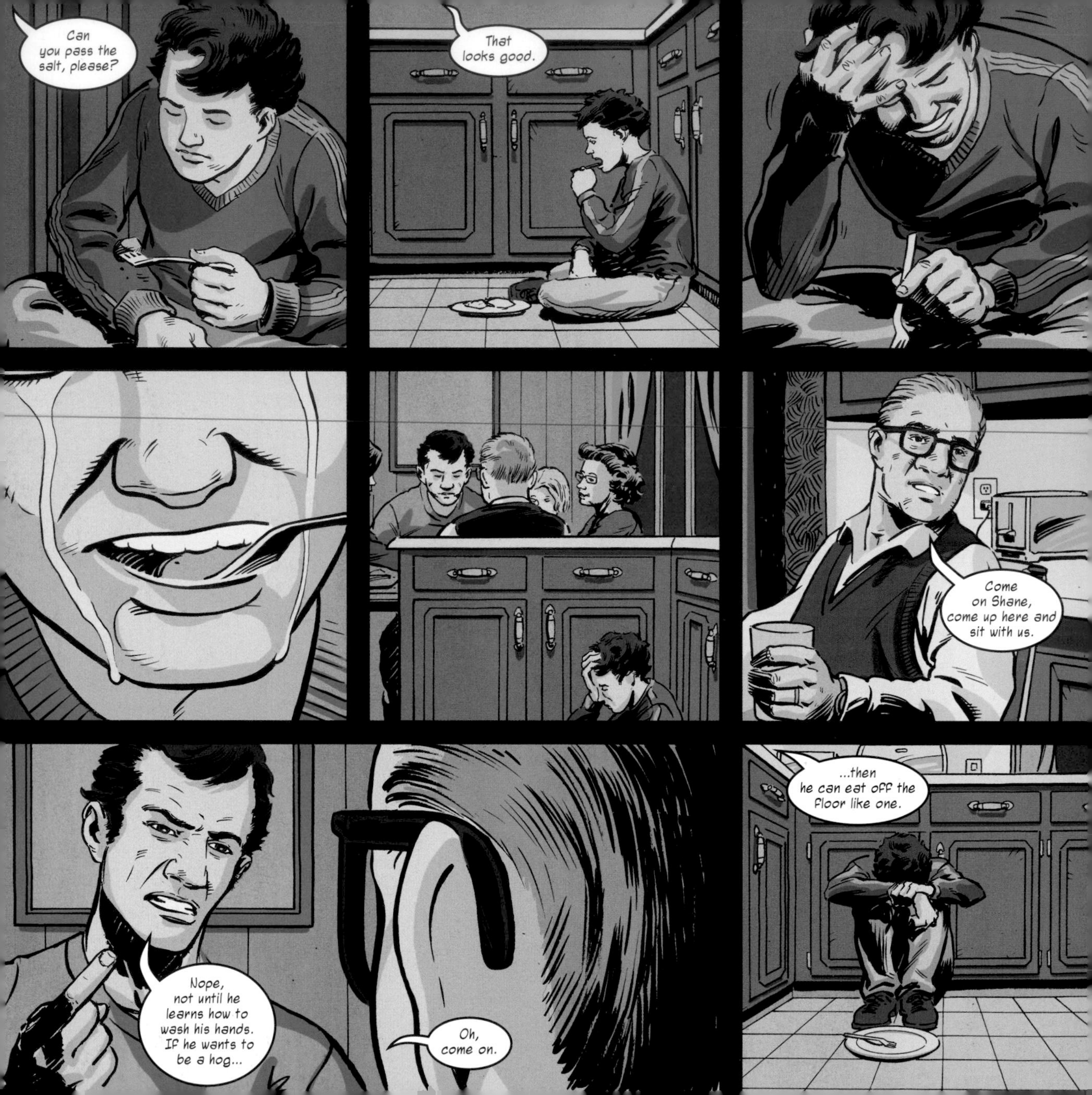
Can you pass the salt, please?
That looks good.
Come on Shane, come up here and sit with us.
Nope, not until he learns how to wash his hands. If he wants to be a hog...
Oh, come on.
...then he can eat off the floor like one.

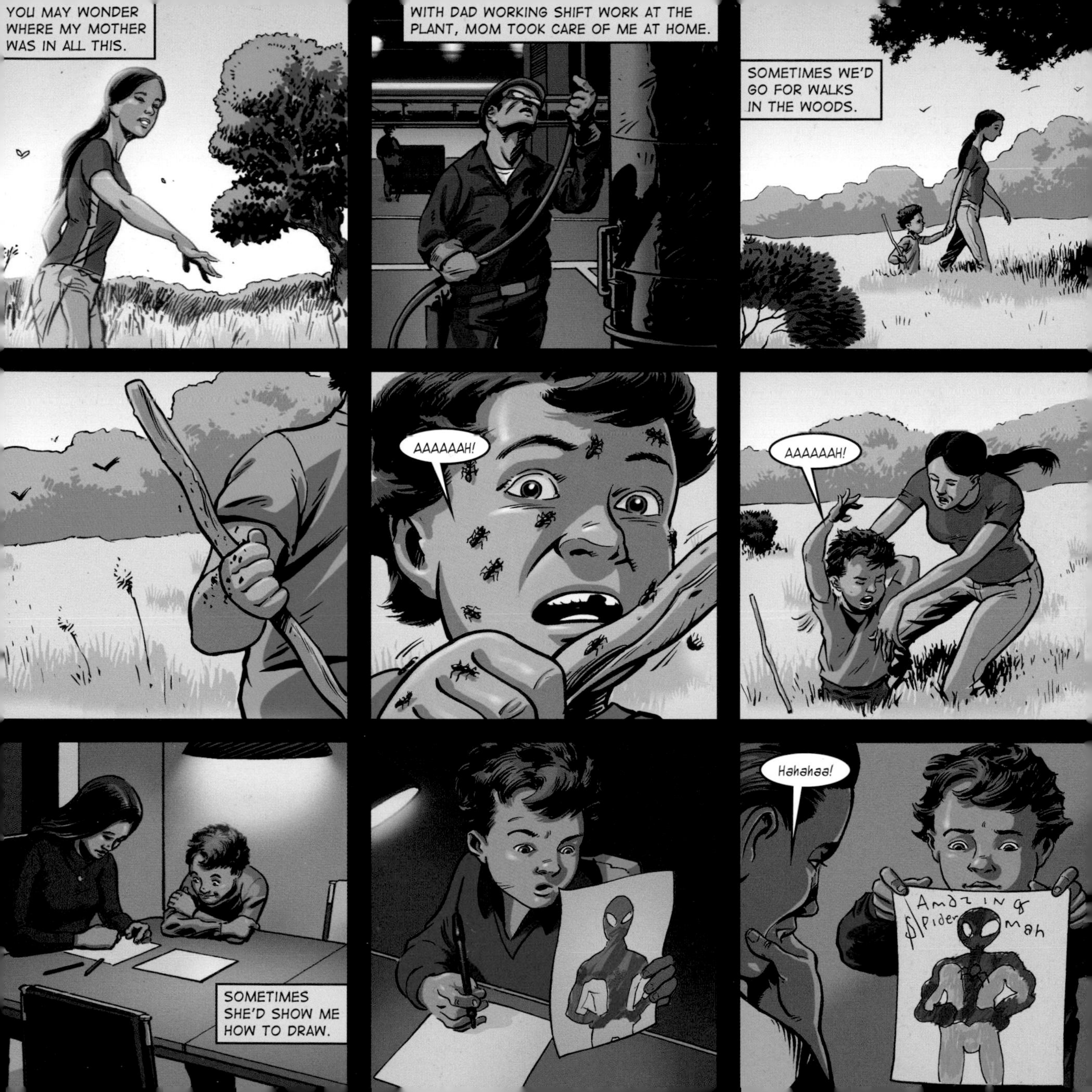
YOU MAY WONDER WHERE MY MOTHER WAS IN ALL THIS.
WITH DAD WORKING SHIFT WORK AT THE PLANT, MOM TOOK CARE OF ME AT HOME.
SOMETIMES WE'D GO FOR WALKS IN THE WOODS.
AAAAAAH!
AAAAAAH!
SOMETIMES SHE'D SHOW ME HOW TO DRAW.
Hahahaa!
Amazing Spider man

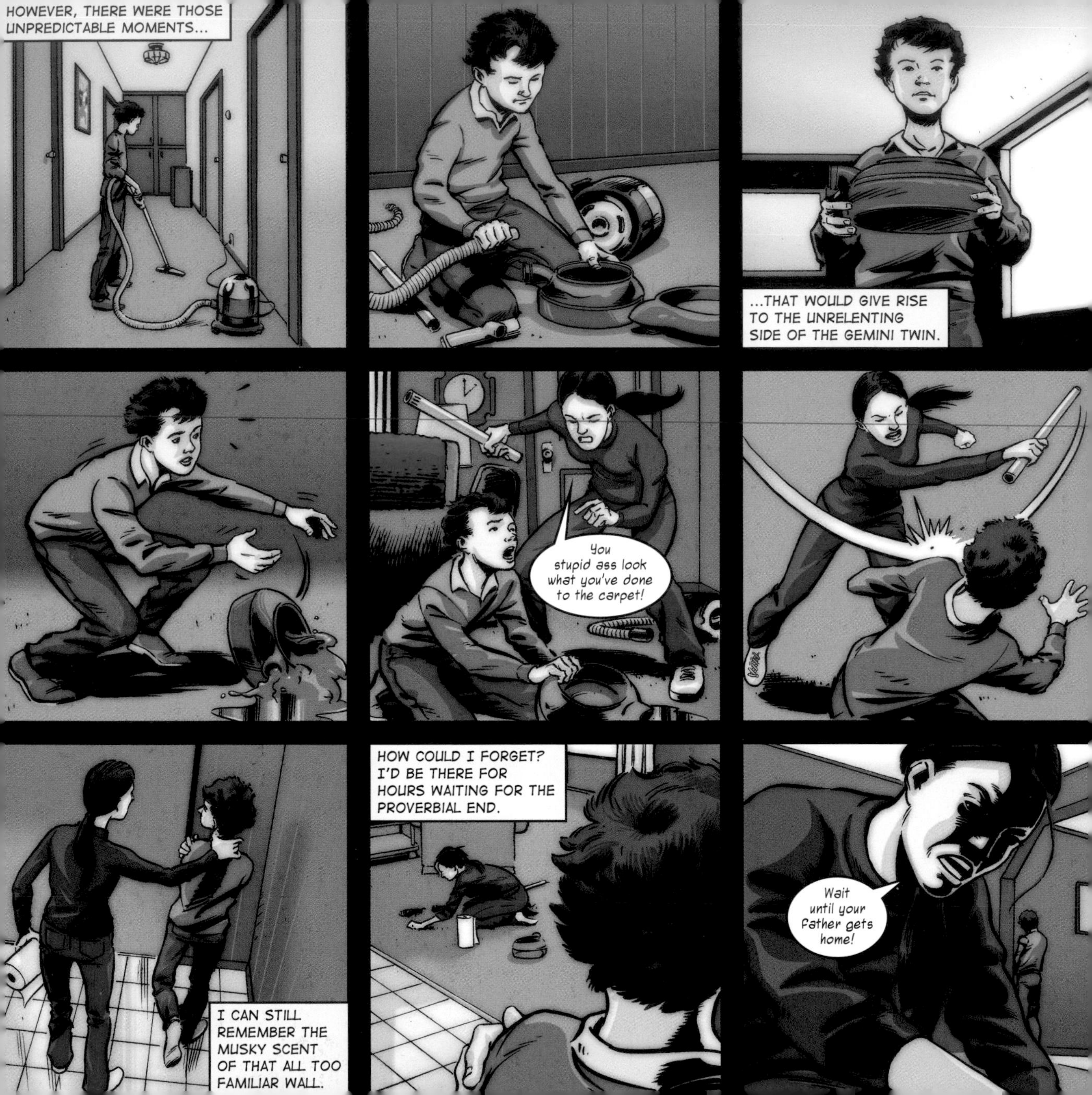
HOWEVER, THERE WERE THOSE UNPREDICTABLE MOMENTS...
...THAT WOULD GIVE RISE TO THE UNRELENTING SIDE OF THE GEMINI TWIN.
You stupid ass look what you've done to the carpet!
I CAN STILL REMEMBER THE MUSKY SCENT OF THAT ALL TOO FAMILIAR WALL.
HOW COULD I FORGET? I'D BE THERE FOR HOURS WAITING FOR THE PROVERBIAL END.
Wait until your father gets home!

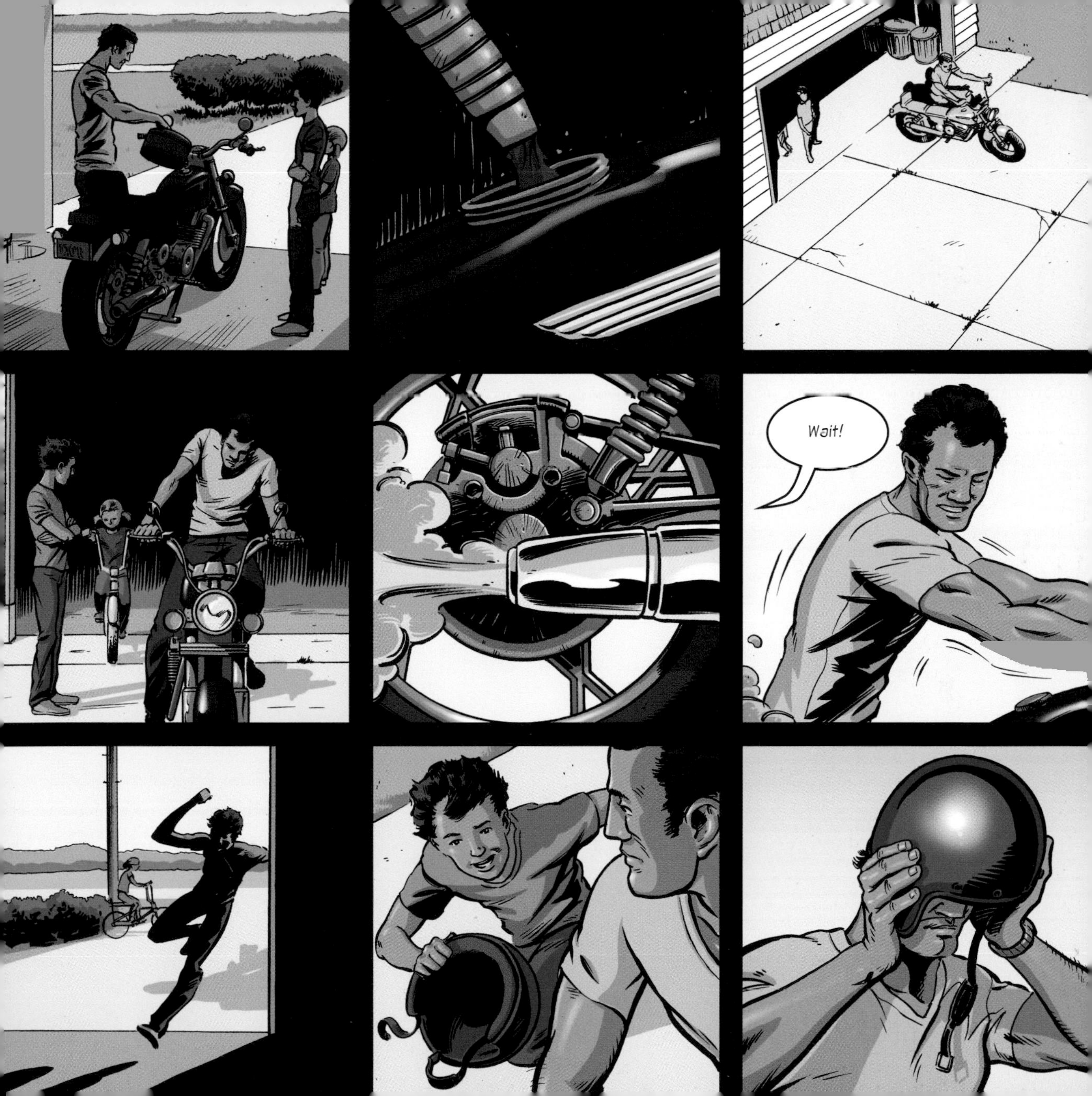
Wait!

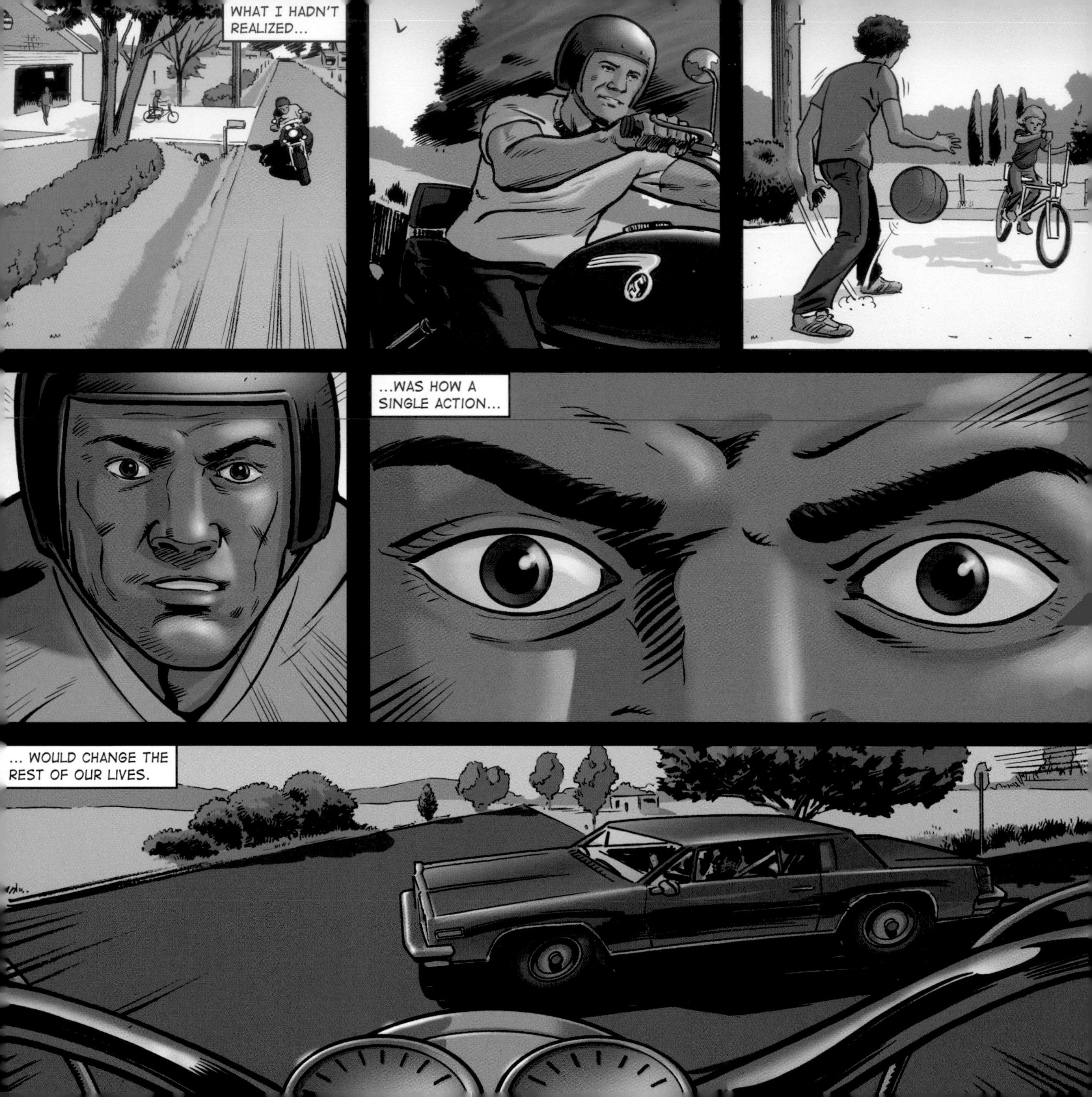
WHAT I HADN'T REALIZED...
...WAS HOW A SINGLE ACTION...
... WOULD CHANGE THE REST OF OUR LIVES.

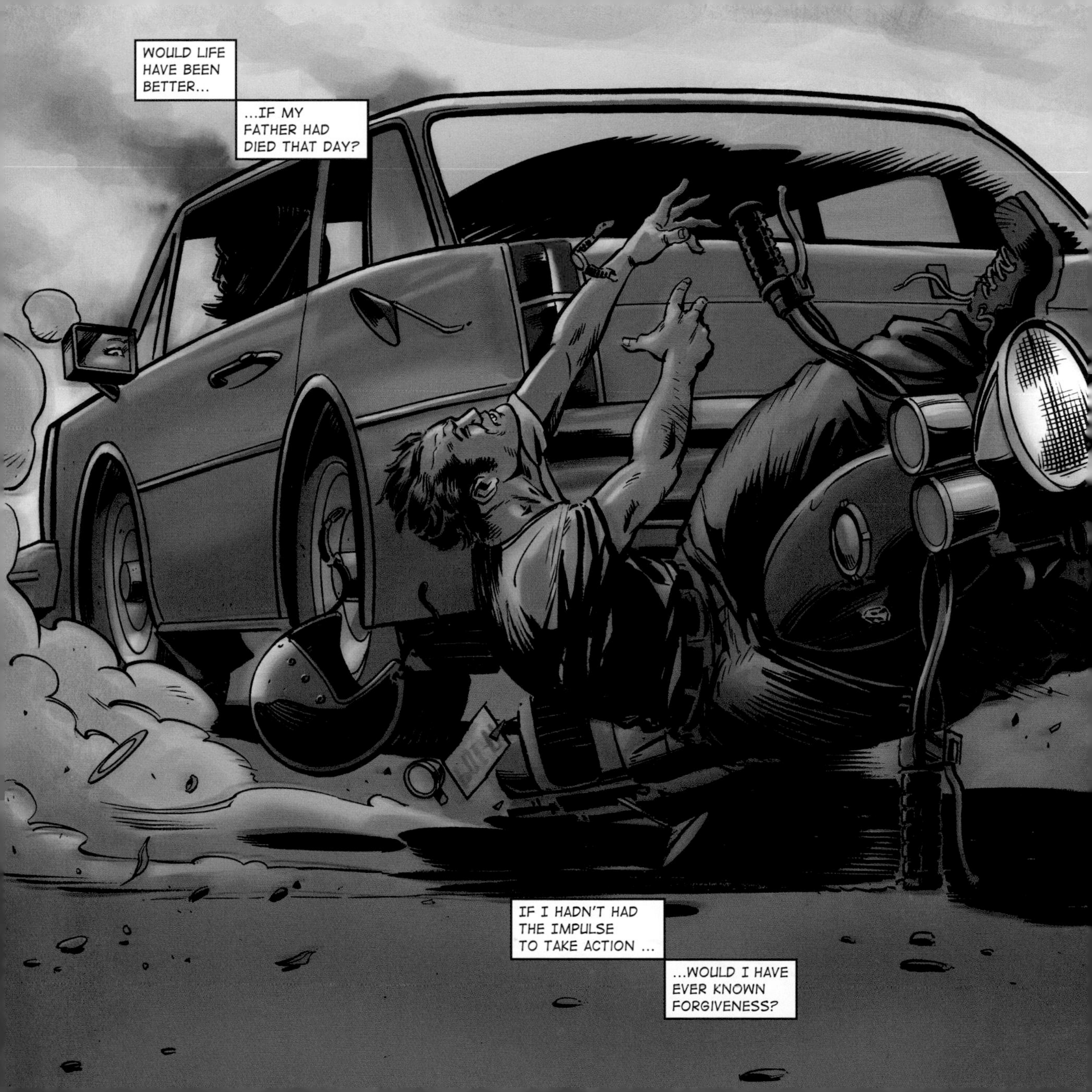
WOULD LIFE HAVE BEEN BETTER...
...IF MY FATHER HAD DIED THAT DAY?
IF I HADN'T HAD THE IMPULSE TO TAKE ACTION ...
...WOULD I HAVE EVER KNOWN FORGIVENESS?

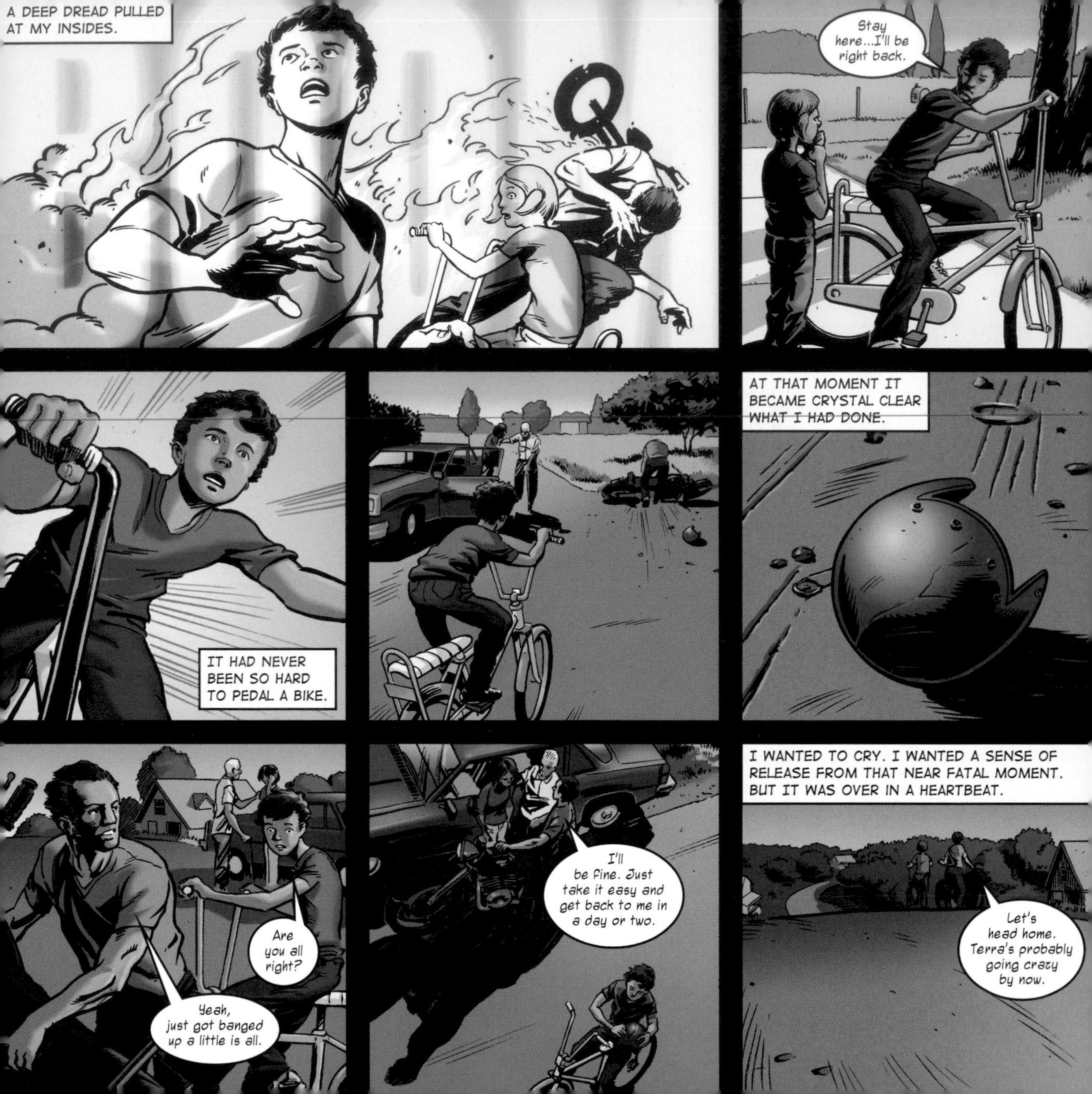

A DEEP DREAD PULLED AT MY INSIDES.
Stay here...I'll be right back.
IT HAD NEVER BEEN SO HARD TO PEDAL A BIKE.
AT THAT MOMENT IT BECAME CRYSTAL CLEAR WHAT I HAD DONE.
Are you all right?
Yeah, just got banged up a little is all.
I'll be fine. Just take it easy and get back to me in a day or two.
I WANTED TO CRY. I WANTED A SENSE OF RELEASE FROM THAT NEAR FATAL MOMENT. BUT IT WAS OVER IN A HEARTBEAT.
Let's head home. Terra's probably going crazy by now.

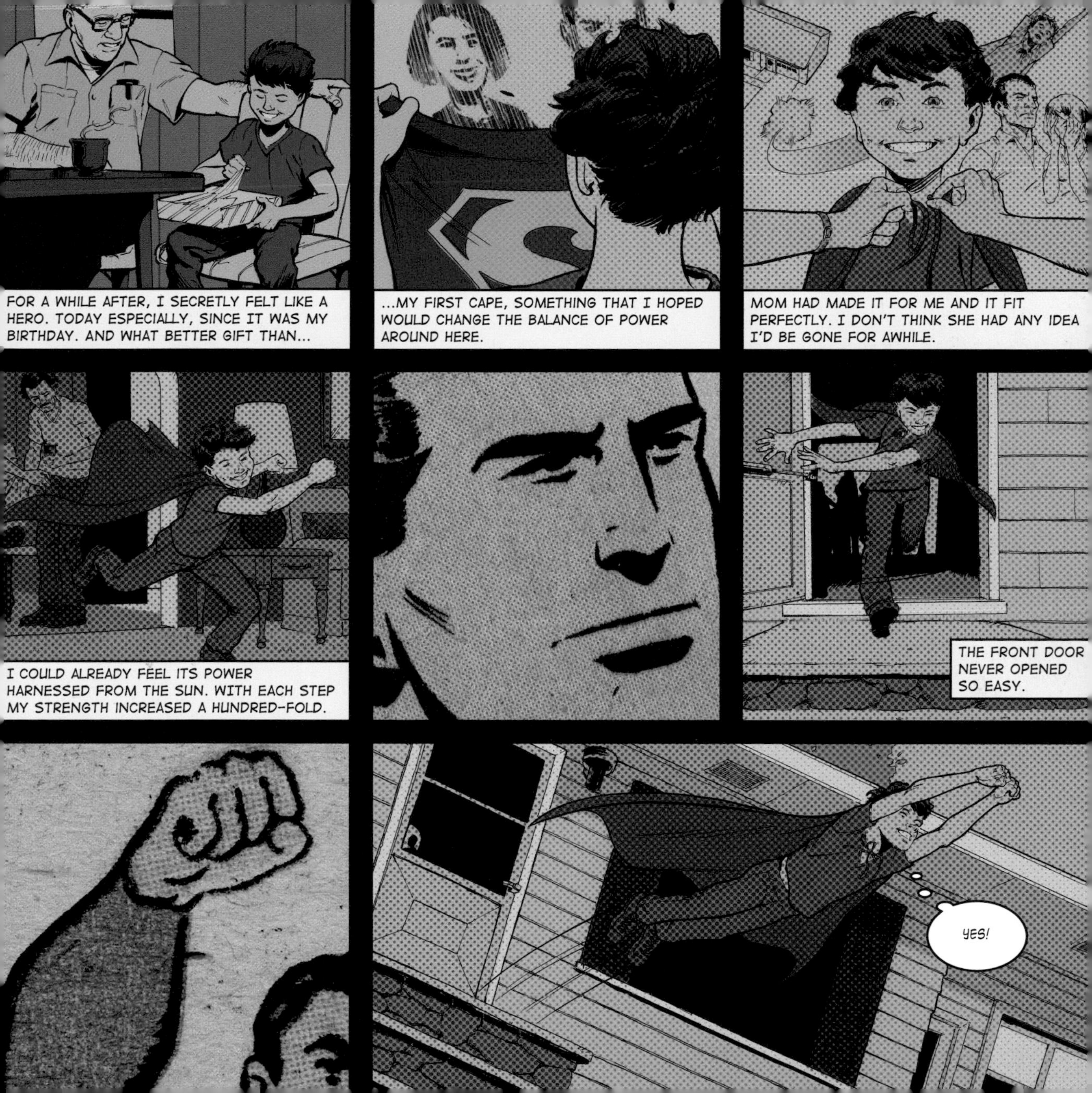
FOR A WHILE AFTER, I SECRETLY FELT LIKE A HERO. TODAY ESPECIALLY, SINCE IT WAS MY BIRTHDAY. AND WHAT BETTER GIFT THAN...
...MY FIRST CAPE, SOMETHING THAT I HOPED WOULD CHANGE THE BALANCE OF POWER AROUND HERE.
MOM HAD MADE IT FOR ME AND IT FIT PERFECTLY. I DON'T THINK SHE HAD ANY IDEA I'D BE GONE FOR AWHILE.
I COULD ALREADY FEEL ITS POWER HARNESSED FROM THE SUN. WITH EACH STEP MY STRENGTH INCREASED A HUNDRED-FOLD.
THE FRONT DOOR NEVER OPENED SO EASY.
YES!

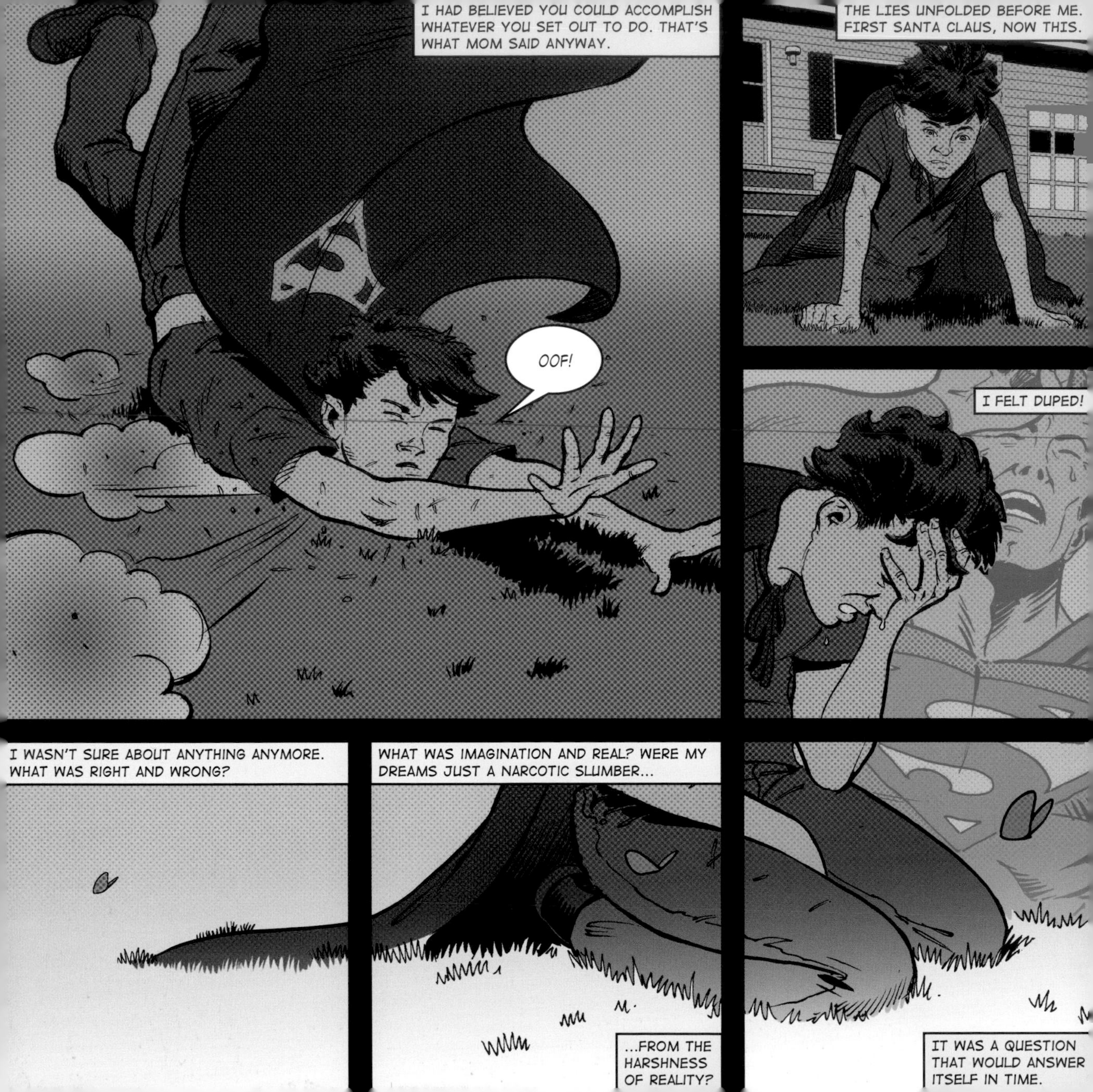
I HAD BELIEVED YOU COULD ACCOMPLISH WHATEVER YOU SET OUT TO DO. THAT'S WHAT MOM SAID ANYWAY.
OOF!
THE LIES UNFOLDED BEFORE ME. FIRST SANTA CLAUS, NOW THIS.
I FELT DUPED!
I WASN'T SURE ABOUT ANYTHING ANYMORE. WHAT WAS RIGHT AND WRONG?
WHAT WAS IMAGINATION AND REAL? WERE MY DREAMS JUST A NARCOTIC SLUMBER...
...FROM THE HARSHNESS OF REALITY?
IT WAS A QUESTION THAT WOULD ANSWER ITSELF IN TIME.

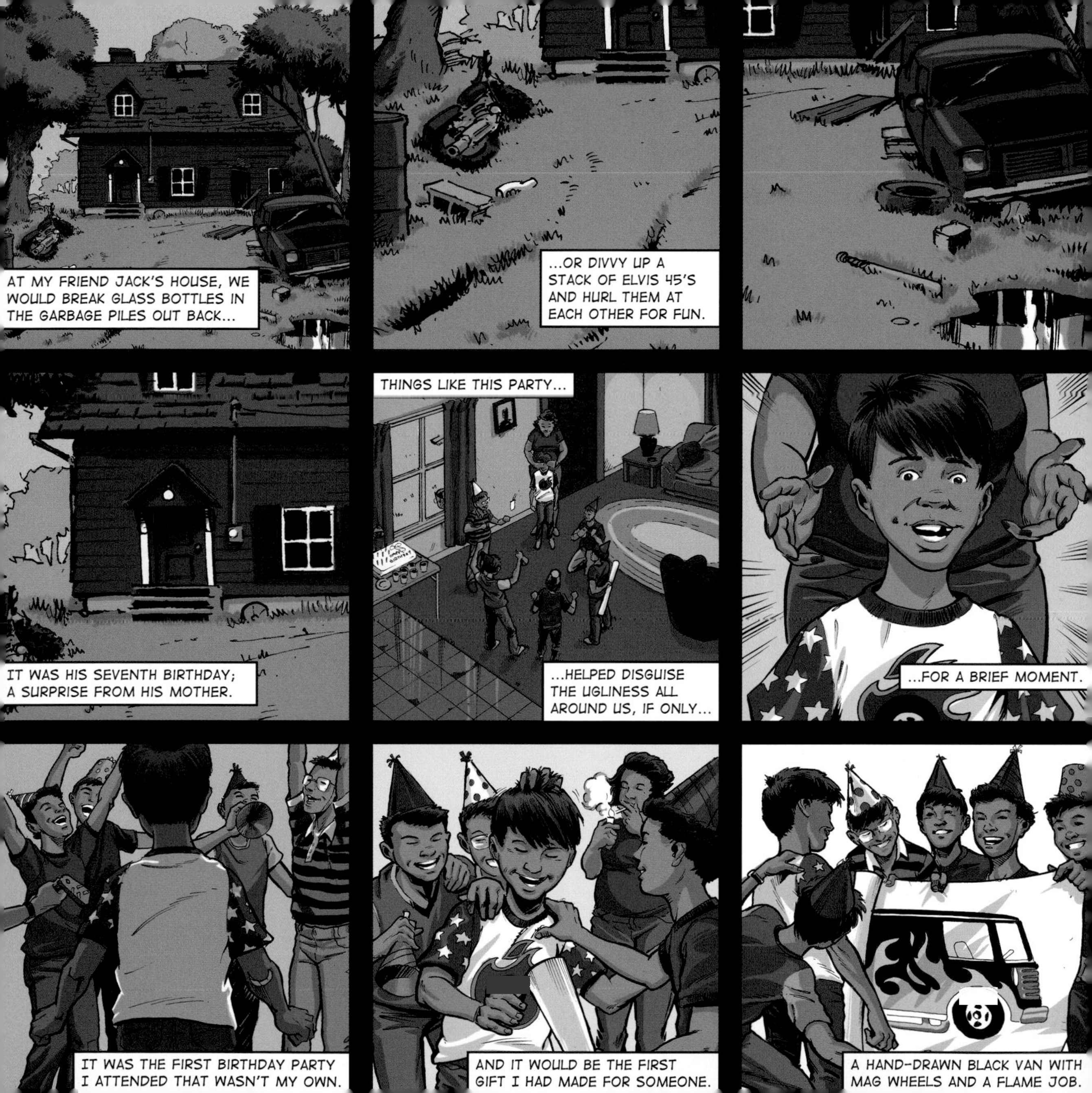
AT MY FRIEND JACK'S HOUSE, WE WOULD BREAK GLASS BOTTLES IN THE GARBAGE PILES OUT BACK...
...OR DIVVY UP A STACK OF ELVIS 45'S AND HURL THEM AT EACH OTHER FOR FUN.
IT WAS HIS SEVENTH BIRTHDAY; A SURPRISE FROM HIS MOTHER.
THINGS LIKE THIS PARTY...
...HELPED DISGUISE THE UGLINESS ALL AROUND US, IF ONLY...
...FOR A BRIEF MOMENT.
IT WAS THE FIRST BIRTHDAY PARTY I ATTENDED THAT WASN'T MY OWN.
AND IT WOULD BE THE FIRST GIFT I HAD MADE FOR SOMEONE.
A HAND-DRAWN BLACK VAN WITH MAG WHEELS AND A FLAME JOB.

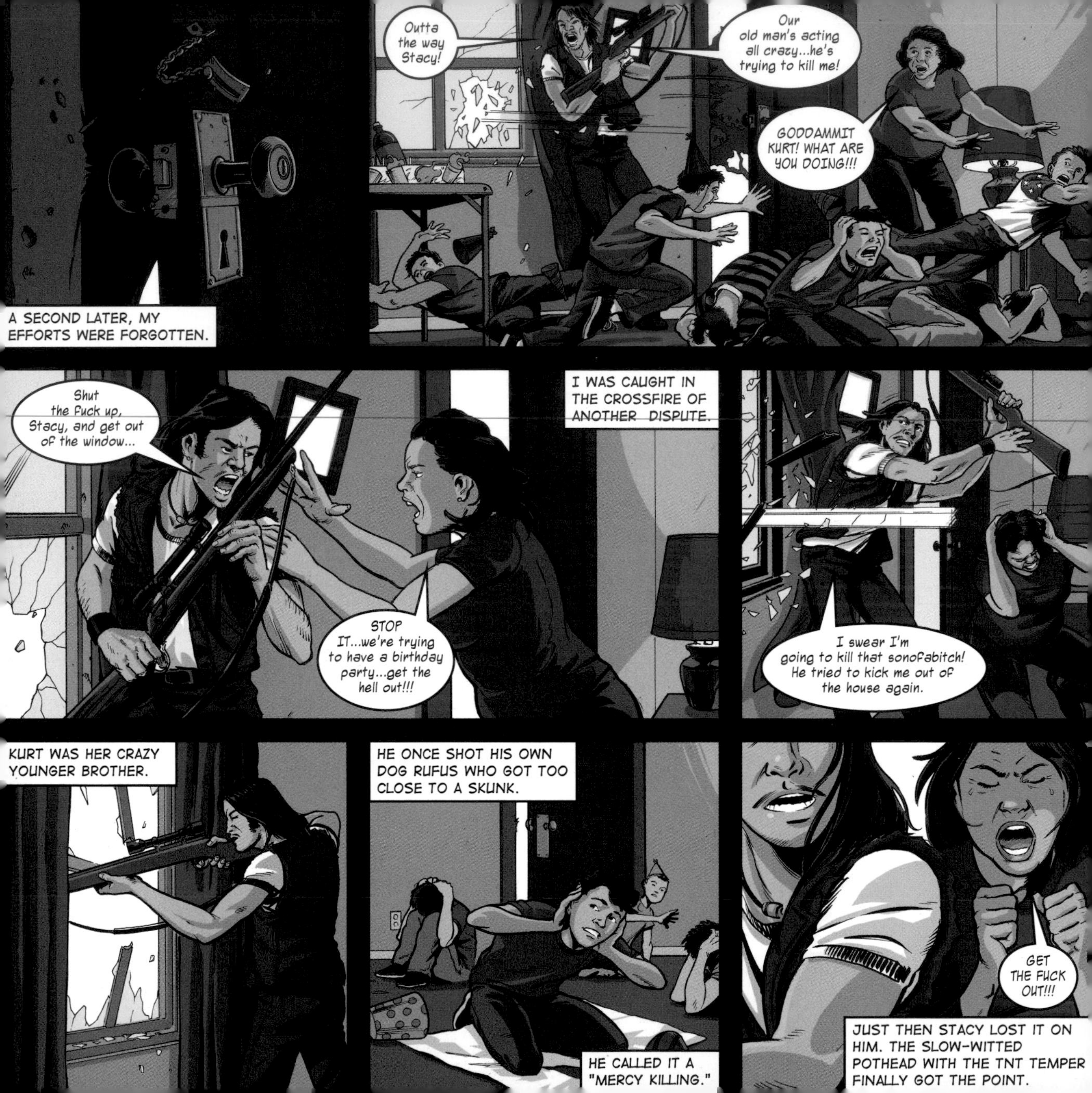
A SECOND LATER, MY EFFORTS WERE FORGOTTEN.
Outta the way Stacy!
Our old man's acting all crazy...he's trying to kill me!
GODDAMMIT KURT! WHAT ARE YOU DOING!!!
Shut the fuck up, Stacy, and get out of the window...
STOP IT...we're trying to have a birthday party...get the hell out!!!
I WAS CAUGHT IN THE CROSSFIRE OF ANOTHER DISPUTE.
I swear I'm going to kill that sonofabitch! He tried to kick me out of the house again.
KURT WAS HER CRAZY YOUNGER BROTHER.
HE ONCE SHOT HIS OWN DOG RUFUS WHO GOT TOO CLOSE TO A SKUNK.
HE CALLED IT A "MERCY KILLING."
GET THE FUCK OUT!!!
JUST THEN STACY LOST IT ON HIM. THE SLOW-WITTED POTHEAD WITH THE TNT TEMPER FINALLY GOT THE POINT.

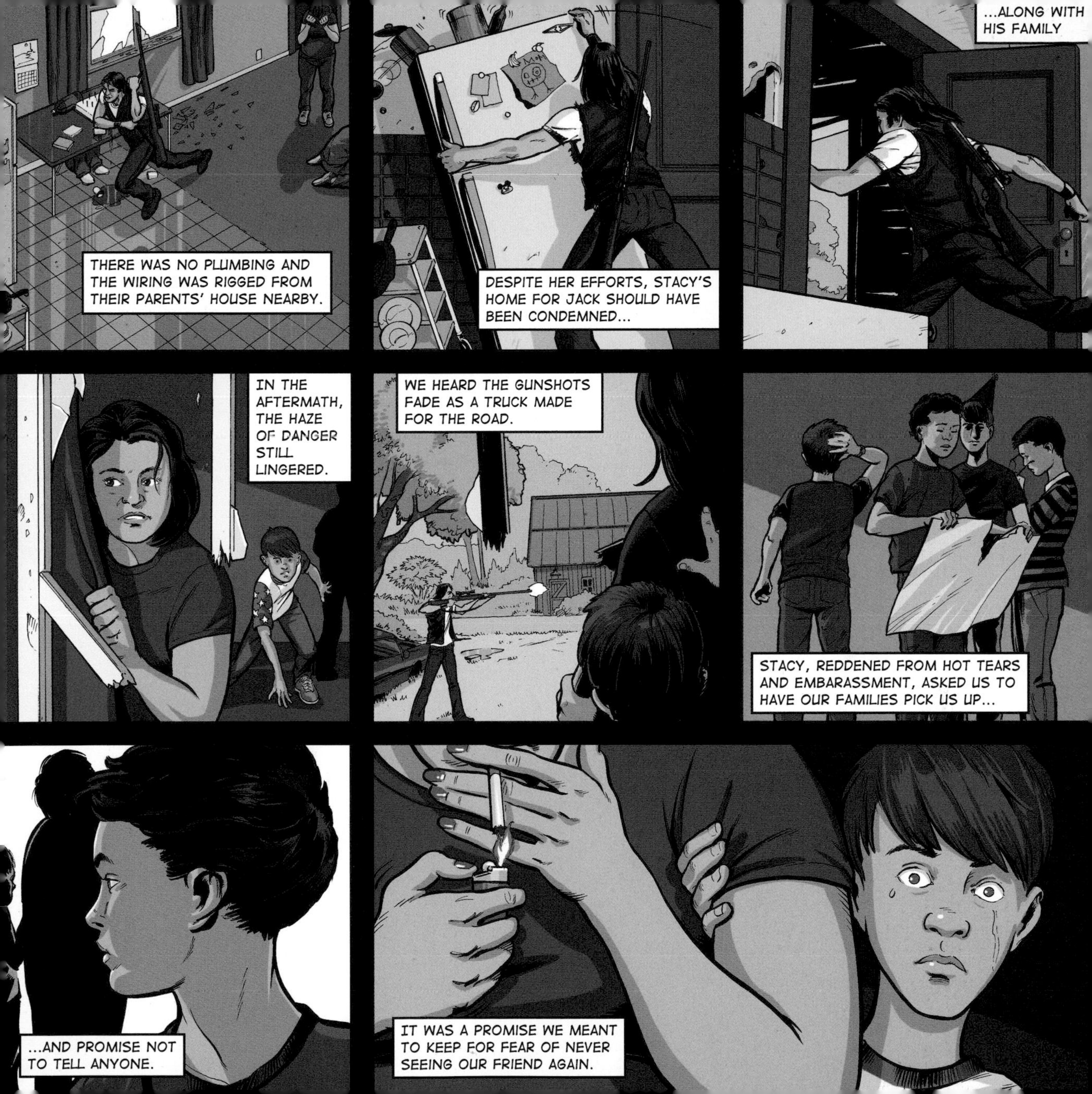
THERE WAS NO PLUMBING AND THE WIRING WAS RIGGED FROM THEIR PARENTS' HOUSE NEARBY.
DESPITE HER EFFORTS, STACY'S HOME FOR JACK SHOULD HAVE BEEN CONDEMNED...
...ALONG WITH HIS FAMILY
IN THE AFTERMATH, THE HAZE OF DANGER STILL LINGERED.
WE HEARD THE GUNSHOTS FADE AS A TRUCK MADE FOR THE ROAD.
STACY, REDDENED FROM HOT TEARS AND EMBARASSMENT, ASKED US TO HAVE OUR FAMILIES PICK US UP...
...AND PROMISE NOT TO TELL ANYONE.
IT WAS A PROMISE WE MEANT TO KEEP FOR FEAR OF NEVER SEEING OUR FRIEND AGAIN.

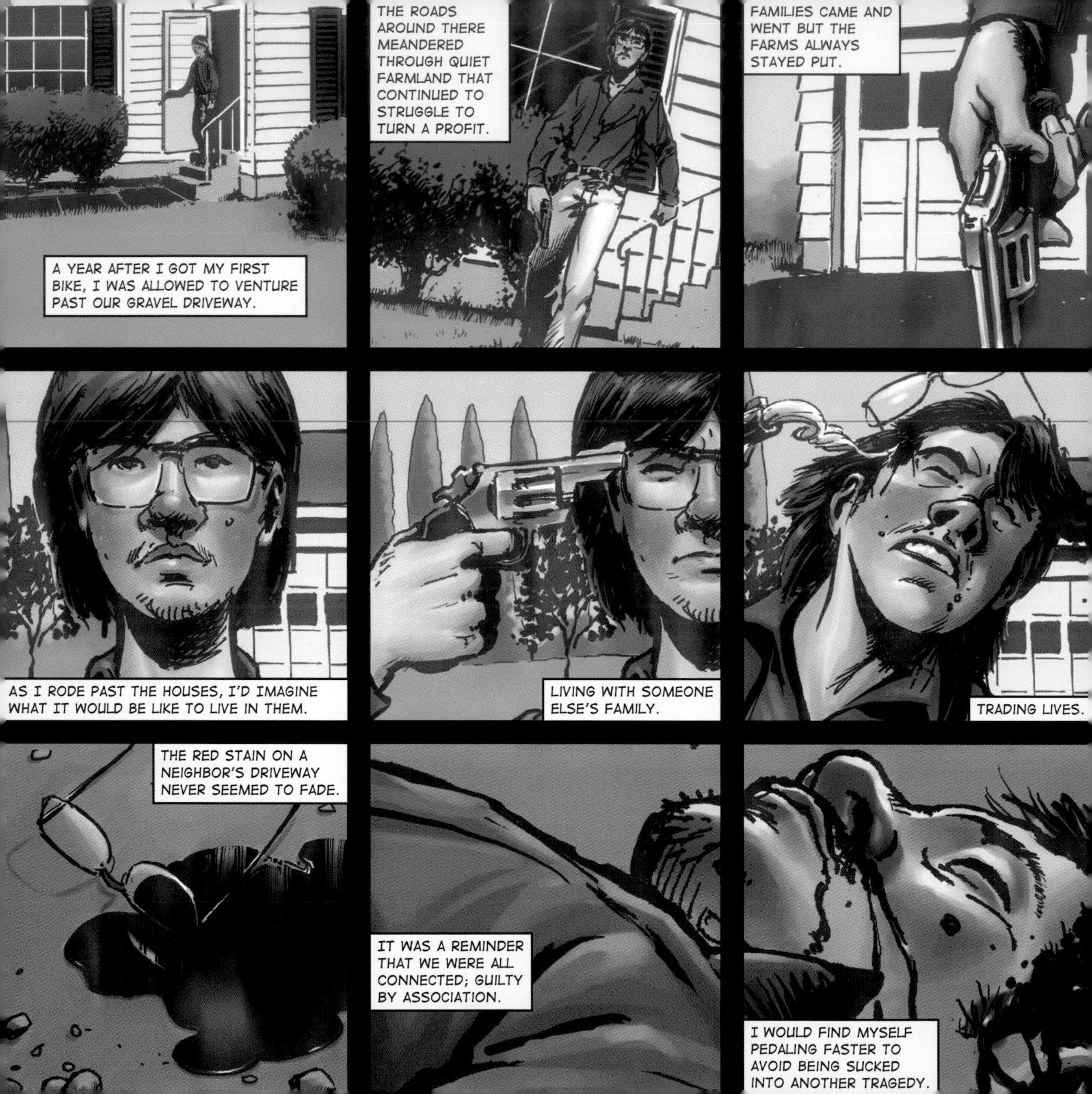
A YEAR AFTER I GOT MY FIRST BIKE, I WAS ALLOWED TO VENTURE PAST OUR GRAVEL DRIVEWAY.
THE ROADS AROUND THERE MEANDERED THROUGH QUIET FARMLAND THAT CONTINUED TO STRUGGLE TO TURN A PROFIT.
FAMILIES CAME AND WENT BUT THE FARMS ALWAYS STAYED PUT.
AS I RODE PAST THE HOUSES, I'D IMAGINE WHAT IT WOULD BE LIKE TO LIVE IN THEM.
LIVING WITH SOMEONE ELSE'S FAMILY.
TRADING LIVES.
THE RED STAIN ON A NEIGHBOR'S DRIVEWAY NEVER SEEMED TO FADE.
IT WAS A REMINDER THAT WE WERE ALL CONNECTED; GUILTY BY ASSOCIATION.
I WOULD FIND MYSELF PEDALING FASTER TO AVOID BEING SUCKED INTO ANOTHER TRAGEDY.

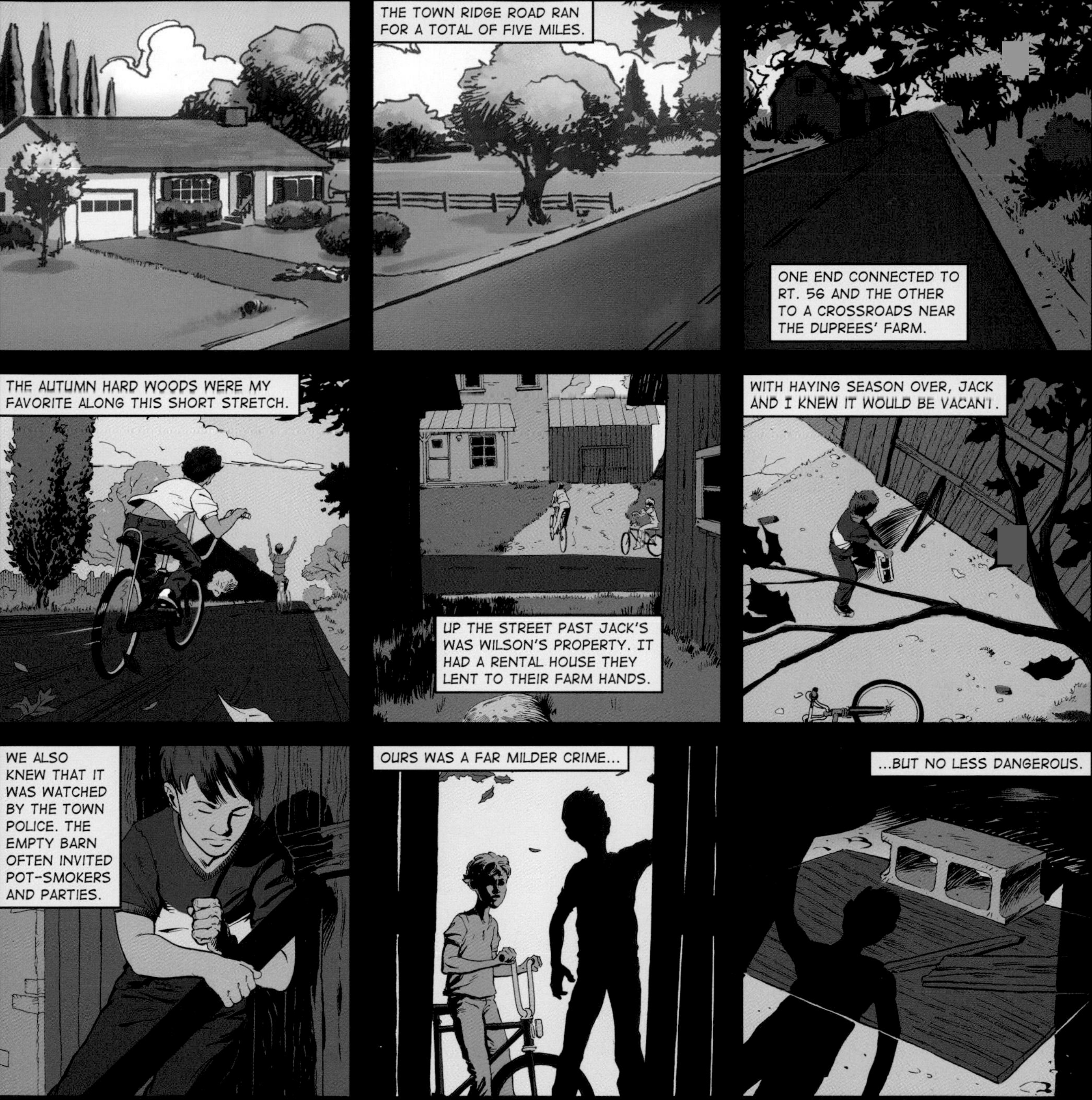
THE TOWN RIDGE ROAD RAN FOR A TOTAL OF FIVE MILES.
ONE END CONNECTED TO RT. 56 AND THE OTHER TO A CROSSROADS NEAR THE DUPREES' FARM.
THE AUTUMN HARD WOODS WERE MY FAVORITE ALONG THIS SHORT STRETCH.
UP THE STREET PAST JACK'S WAS WILSON'S PROPERTY. IT HAD A RENTAL HOUSE THEY LENT TO THEIR FARM HANDS.
WITH HAYING SEASON OVER, JACK AND I KNEW IT WOULD BE VACANT.
WE ALSO KNEW THAT IT WAS WATCHED BY THE TOWN POLICE. THE EMPTY BARN OFTEN INVITED POT-SMOKERS AND PARTIES.
OURS WAS A FAR MILDER CRIME...
...BUT NO LESS DANGEROUS.

WHEN I WASN'T WORKING WITH MY DAD, JACK AND I WOULD RIDE OUR BIKES EVERYWHERE OR PLAY WITH HOTWHEELS.

OUR FAVORITE CARS WERE TRANS AMS. OUR FAVORITE MOVIES: SMOKEY AND THE BANDIT PARTS I AND II... III SUCKED!

THEN WE SAW "HOOPER". THAT'S WHEN WE DECIDED TO BECOME STUNTMEN.

AHHHHHH!

THE SUN-DRENCHED ROAD SOOTHED MY YET DISCOVERED INJURIES... BURT REYNOLDS WAS CLEARLY THE BETTER STUNTMAN.

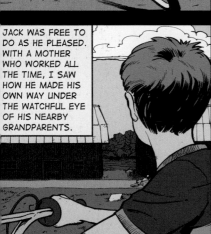

JACK WAS FREE TO DO AS HE PLEASED. WITH A MOTHER WHO WORKED ALL THE TIME, I SAW HOW HE MADE HIS OWN WAY UNDER THE WATCHFUL EYE OF HIS NEARBY GRANDPARENTS.

WITH HIM I COULD TEAR AROUND AND BE A KID...

...WITHOUT THE UNJUST CONSEQUENCES THAT LIVED UNDER MY ROOF.

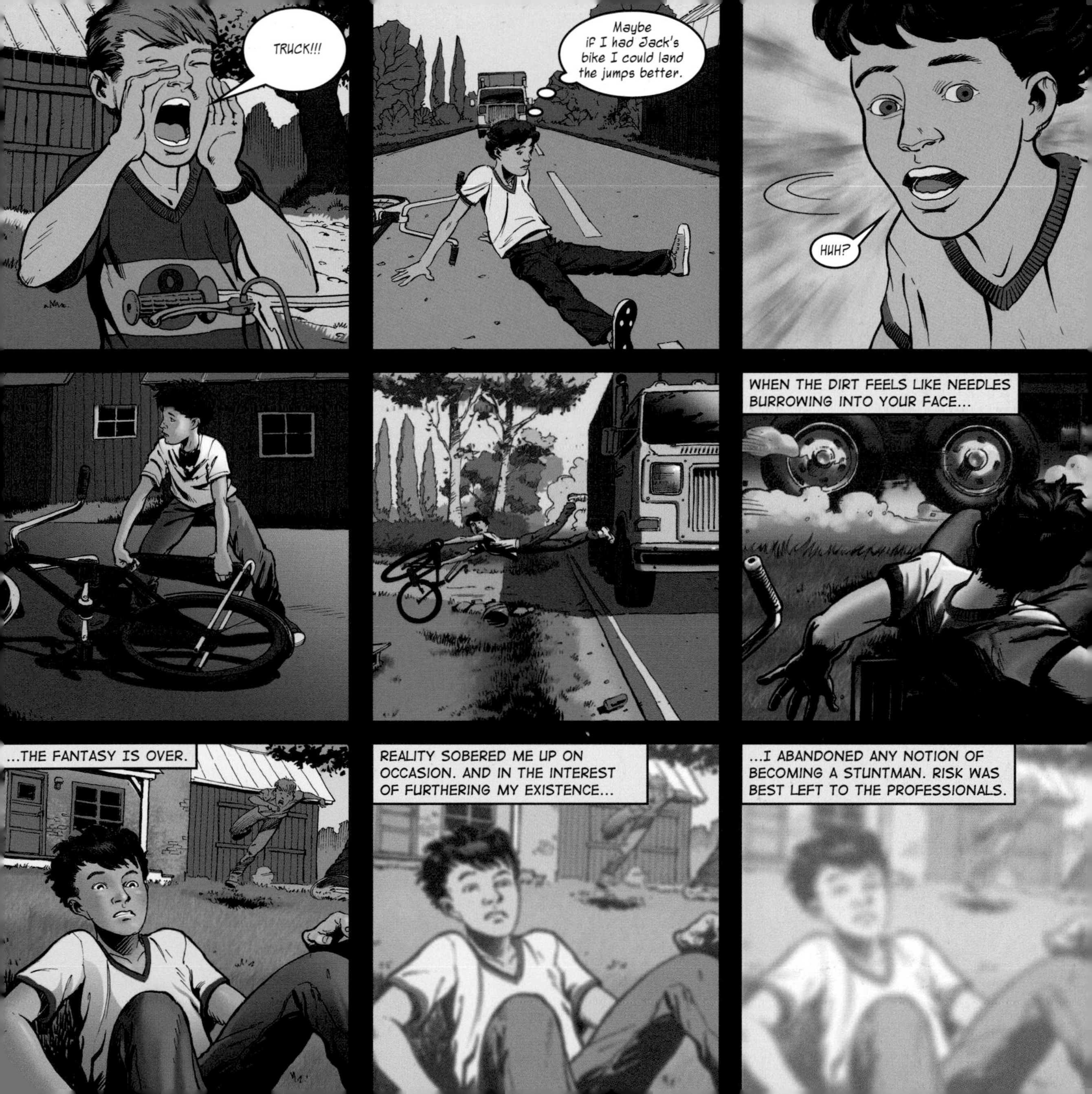
TRUCK!!!
Maybe if I had Jack's bike I could land the jumps better.
HUH?
WHEN THE DIRT FEELS LIKE NEEDLES BURROWING INTO YOUR FACE...
...THE FANTASY IS OVER.
REALITY SOBERED ME UP ON OCCASION. AND IN THE INTEREST OF FURTHERING MY EXISTENCE...
...I ABANDONED ANY NOTION OF BECOMING A STUNTMAN. RISK WAS BEST LEFT TO THE PROFESSIONALS.

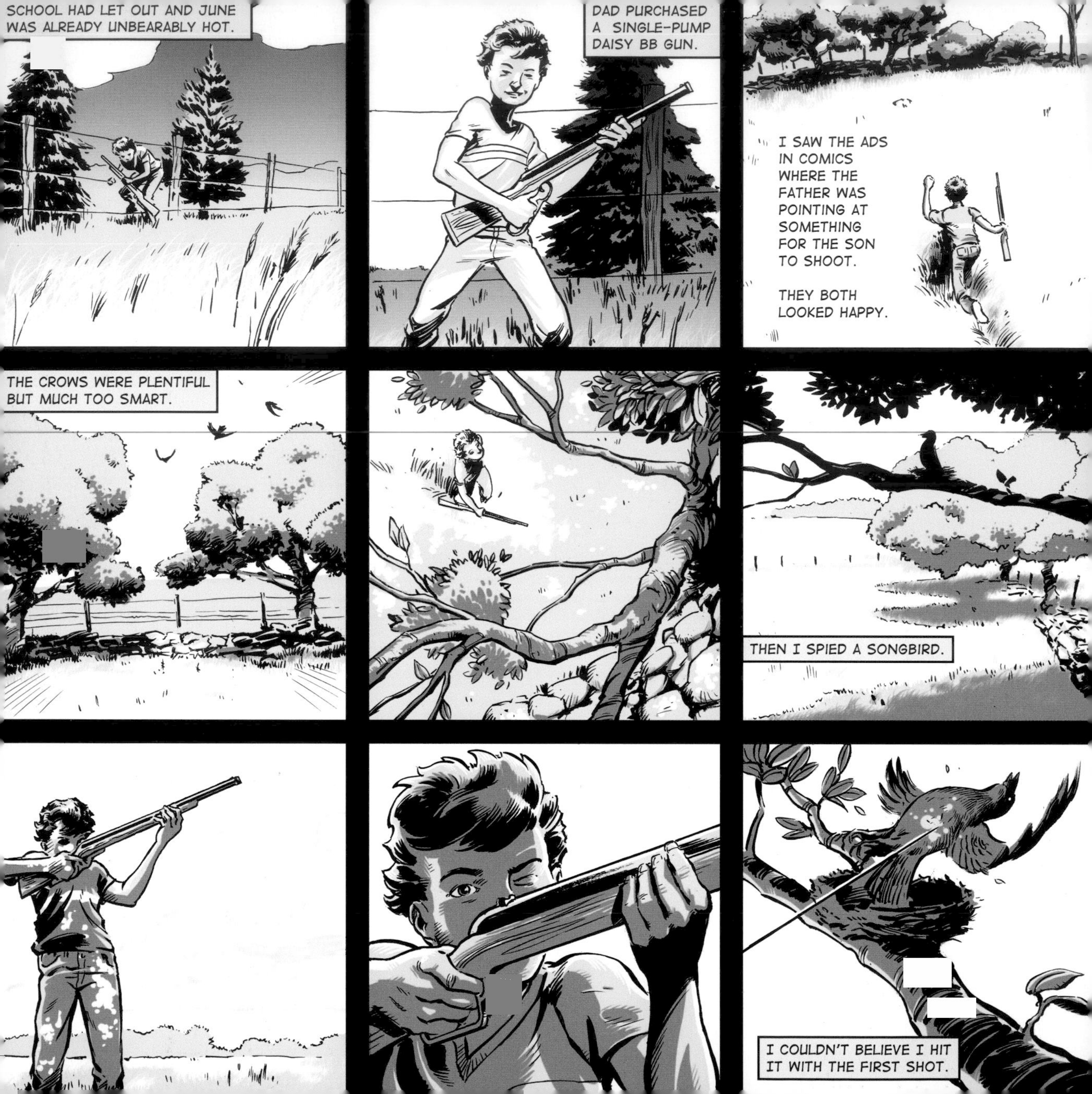
SCHOOL HAD LET OUT AND JUNE WAS ALREADY UNBEARABLY HOT.
DAD PURCHASED A SINGLE-PUMP DAISY BB GUN.
I SAW THE ADS IN COMICS WHERE THE FATHER WAS POINTING AT SOMETHING FOR THE SON TO SHOOT.
THEY BOTH LOOKED HAPPY.
THE CROWS WERE PLENTIFUL BUT MUCH TOO SMART.
THEN I SPIED A SONGBIRD.
I COULDN'T BELIEVE I HIT IT WITH THE FIRST SHOT.

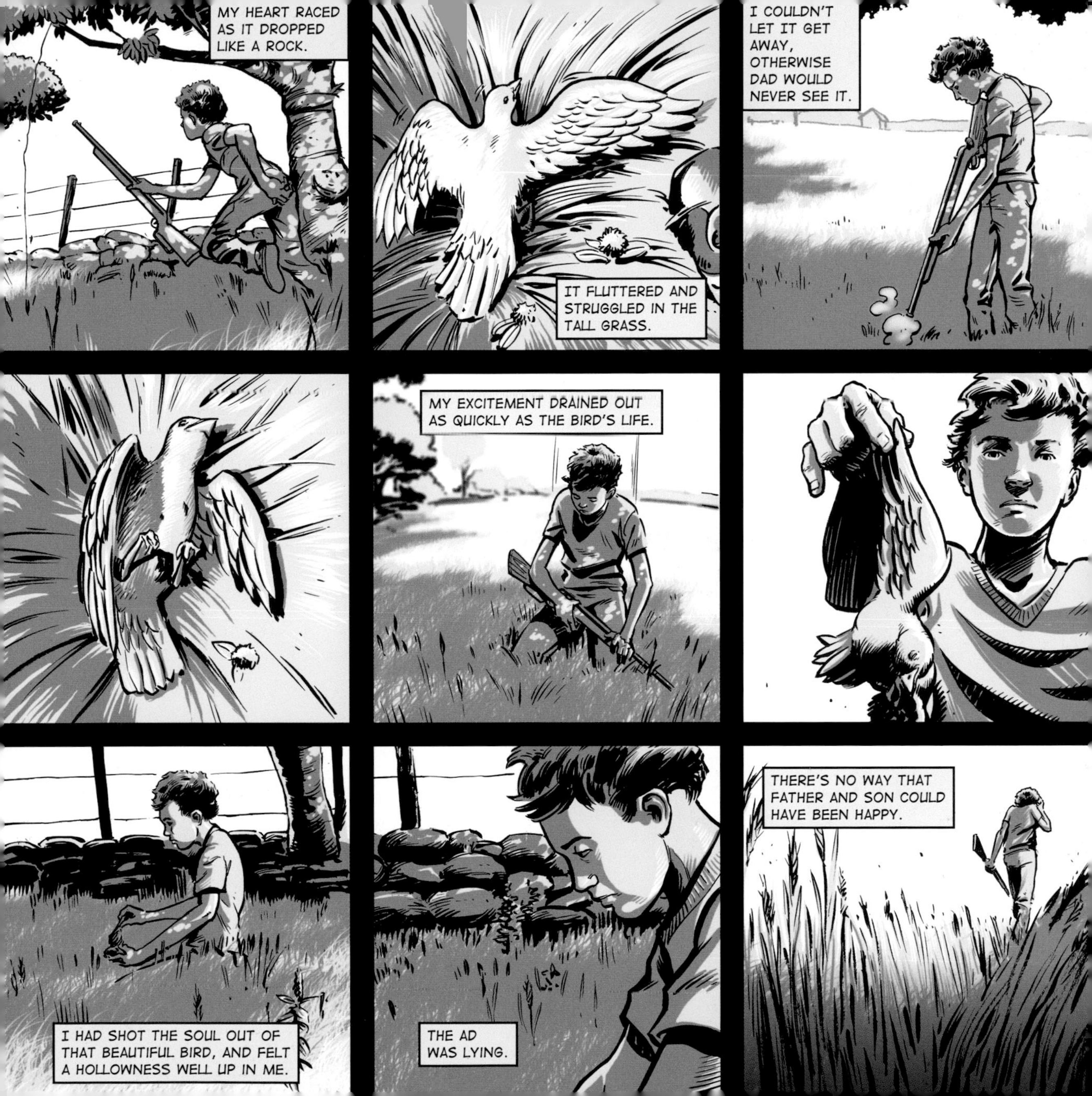
MY HEART RACED AS IT DROPPED LIKE A ROCK.
IT FLUTTERED AND STRUGGLED IN THE TALL GRASS.
I COULDN'T LET IT GET AWAY, OTHERWISE DAD WOULD NEVER SEE IT.
MY EXCITEMENT DRAINED OUT AS QUICKLY AS THE BIRD'S LIFE.
I HAD SHOT THE SOUL OUT OF THAT BEAUTIFUL BIRD, AND FELT A HOLLOWNESS WELL UP IN ME.
THE AD WAS LYING.
THERE'S NO WAY THAT FATHER AND SON COULD HAVE BEEN HAPPY.

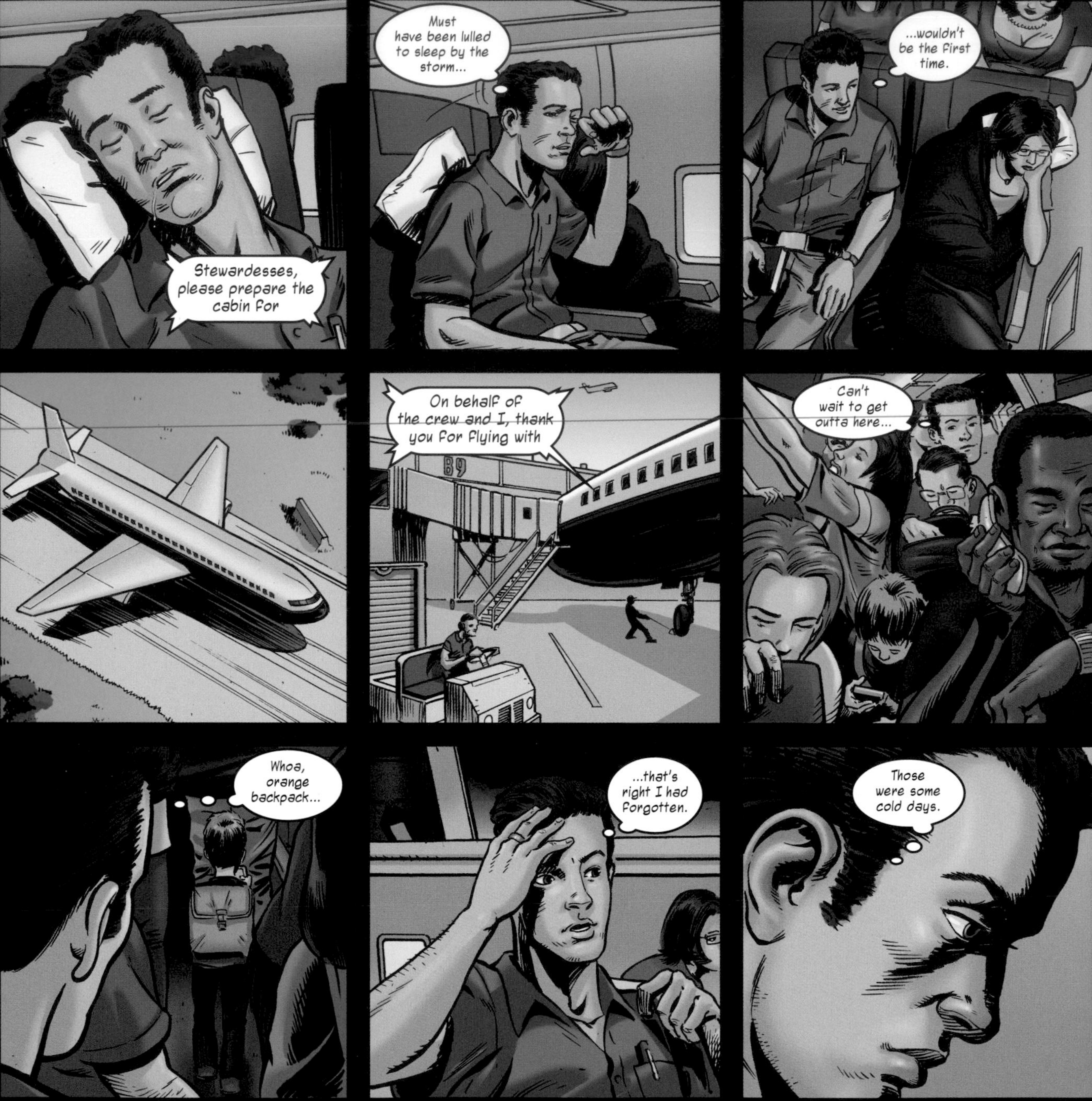
Stewardesses, please prepare the cabin for
Must have been lulled to sleep by the storm...
...wouldn't be the first time.
On behalf of the crew and I, thank you for flying with
B9
Can't wait to get outta here...
Whoa, orange backpack...
...that's right I had forgotten.
Those were some cold days.

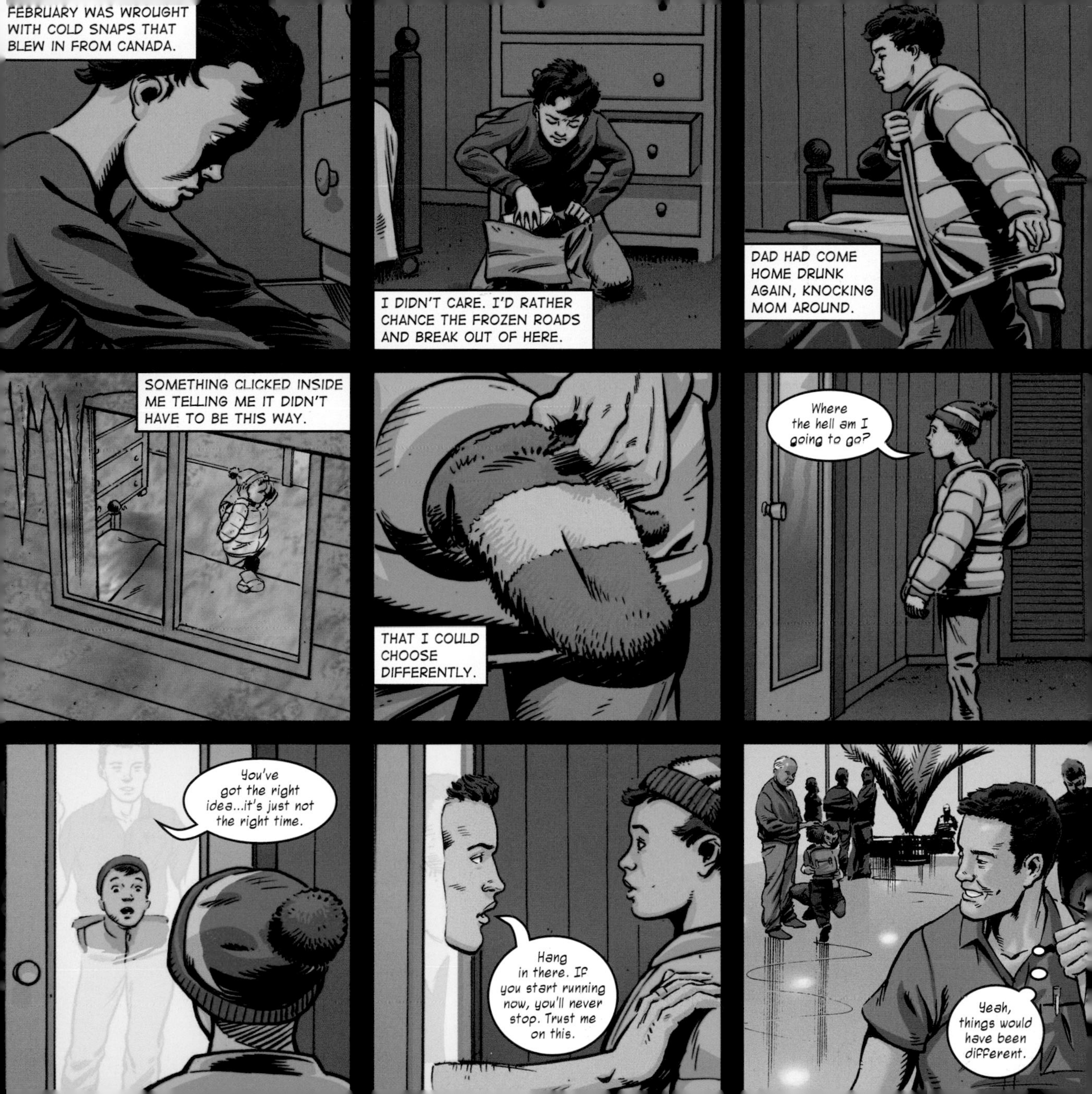
FEBRUARY WAS WROUGHT WITH COLD SNAPS THAT BLEW IN FROM CANADA.
I DIDN'T CARE. I'D RATHER CHANCE THE FROZEN ROADS AND BREAK OUT OF HERE.
DAD HAD COME HOME DRUNK AGAIN, KNOCKING MOM AROUND.
SOMETHING CLICKED INSIDE ME TELLING ME IT DIDN'T HAVE TO BE THIS WAY.
THAT I COULD CHOOSE DIFFERENTLY.
Where the hell am I going to go?
You've got the right idea...it's just not the right time.
Hang in there. If you start running now, you'll never stop. Trust me on this.
Yeah, things would have been different.

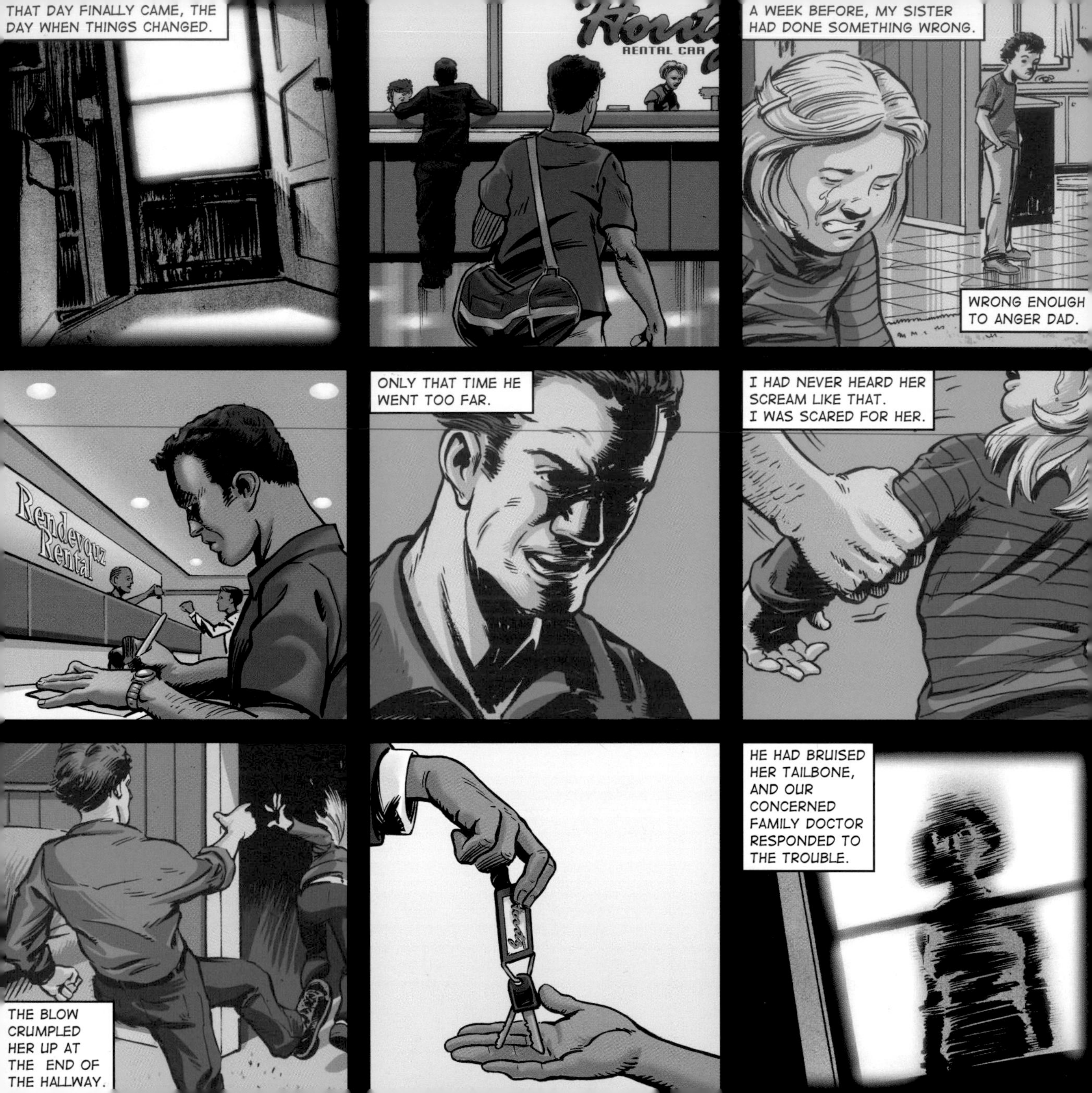
THAT DAY FINALLY CAME, THE DAY WHEN THINGS CHANGED.
RENTAL CAR
A WEEK BEFORE, MY SISTER HAD DONE SOMETHING WRONG.
WRONG ENOUGH TO ANGER DAD.
Rendevouz Rental
ONLY THAT TIME HE WENT TOO FAR.
I HAD NEVER HEARD HER SCREAM LIKE THAT. I WAS SCARED FOR HER.
THE BLOW CRUMPLED HER UP AT THE END OF THE HALLWAY.
HE HAD BRUISED HER TAILBONE, AND OUR CONCERNED FAMILY DOCTOR RESPONDED TO THE TROUBLE.

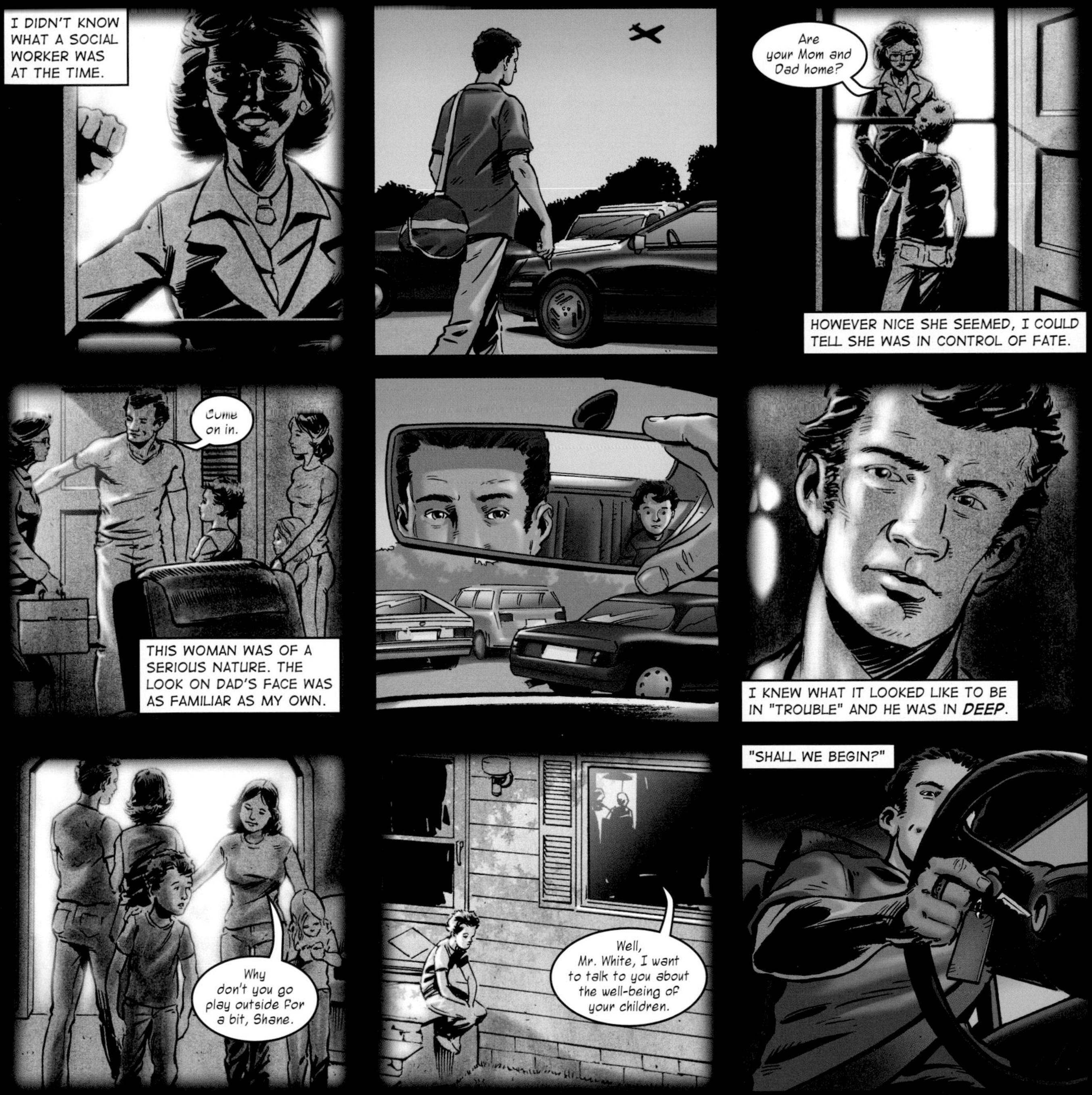
I DIDN'T KNOW WHAT A SOCIAL WORKER WAS AT THE TIME.
Are your Mom and Dad home?
HOWEVER NICE SHE SEEMED, I COULD TELL SHE WAS IN CONTROL OF FATE.
Come on in.
THIS WOMAN WAS OF A SERIOUS NATURE. THE LOOK ON DAD'S FACE WAS AS FAMILIAR AS MY OWN.
I KNEW WHAT IT LOOKED LIKE TO BE IN "TROUBLE" AND HE WAS IN *DEEP*.
Why don't you go play outside for a bit, Shane.
Well, Mr. White, I want to talk to you about the well-being of your children.
"SHALL WE BEGIN?"

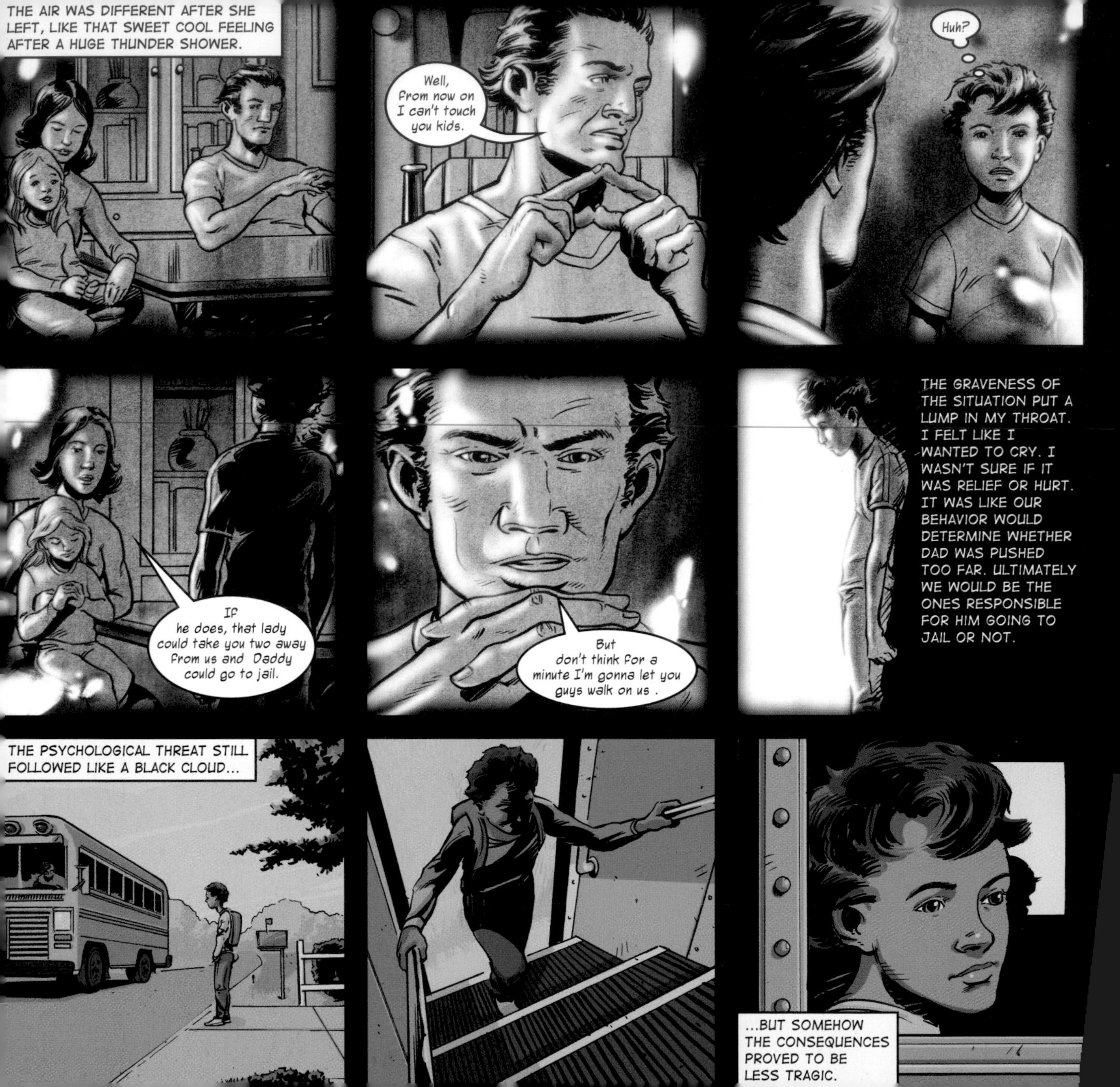
THE AIR WAS DIFFERENT AFTER SHE LEFT, LIKE THAT SWEET COOL FEELING AFTER A HUGE THUNDER SHOWER.
Well, From now on I can't touch you kids.
Huh?
If he does, that lady could take you two away from us and Daddy could go to jail.
But don't think for a minute I'm gonna let you guys walk on us .
THE GRAVENESS OF THE SITUATION PUT A LUMP IN MY THROAT. I FELT LIKE I WANTED TO CRY. I WASN'T SURE IF IT WAS RELIEF OR HURT. IT WAS LIKE OUR BEHAVIOR WOULD DETERMINE WHETHER DAD WAS PUSHED TOO FAR. ULTIMATELY WE WOULD BE THE ONES RESPONSIBLE FOR HIM GOING TO JAIL OR NOT.
THE PSYCHOLOGICAL THREAT STILL FOLLOWED LIKE A BLACK CLOUD...
...BUT SOMEHOW THE CONSEQUENCES PROVED TO BE LESS TRAGIC.

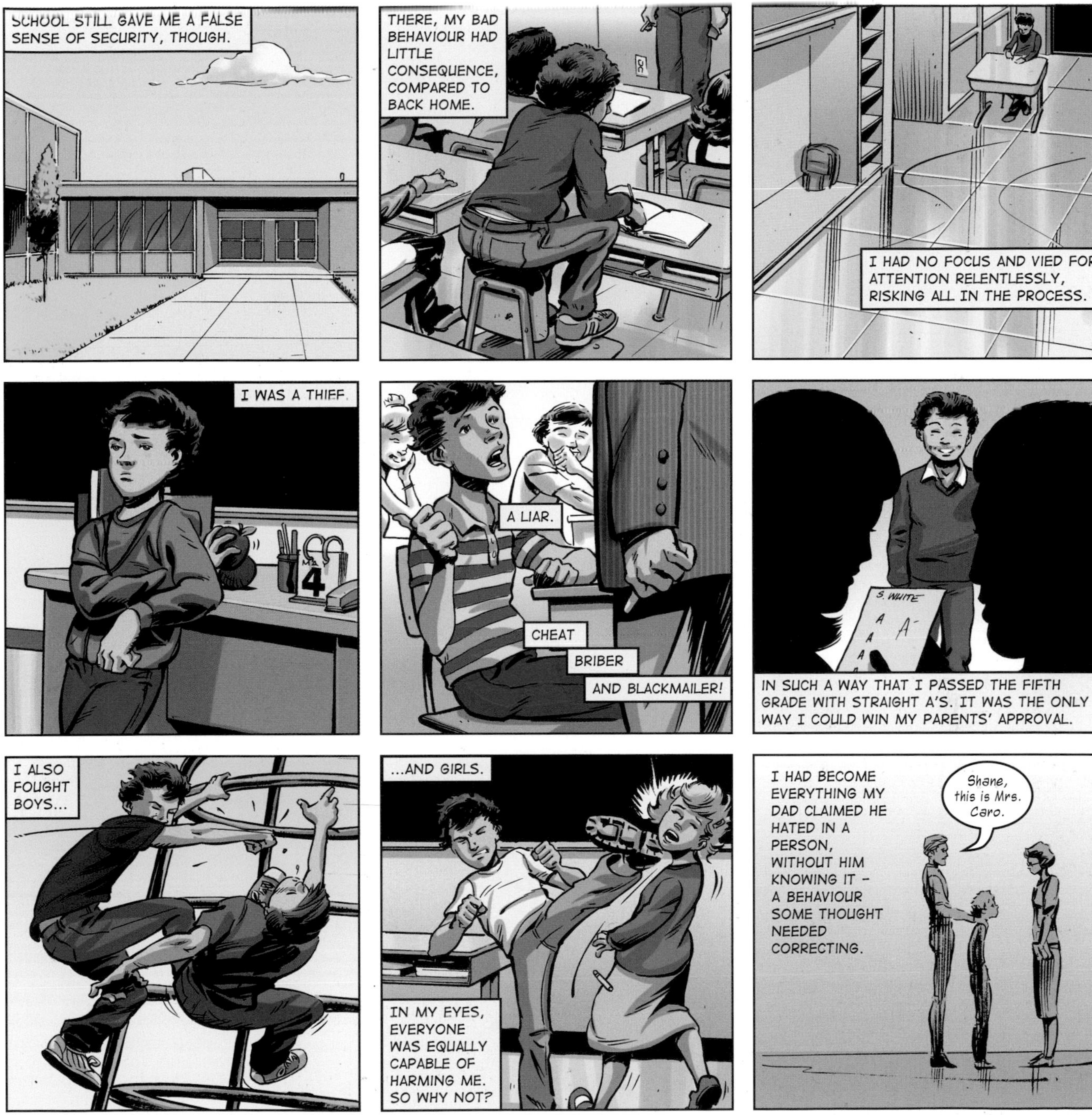
SCHOOL STILL GAVE ME A FALSE SENSE OF SECURITY, THOUGH.
THERE, MY BAD BEHAVIOUR HAD LITTLE CONSEQUENCE, COMPARED TO BACK HOME.
I HAD NO FOCUS AND VIED FOR ATTENTION RELENTLESSLY, RISKING ALL IN THE PROCESS.
I WAS A THIEF.
A LIAR.
CHEAT
BRIBER
AND BLACKMAILER!
S. WHITE
IN SUCH A WAY THAT I PASSED THE FIFTH GRADE WITH STRAIGHT A'S. IT WAS THE ONLY WAY I COULD WIN MY PARENTS' APPROVAL.
I ALSO FOUGHT BOYS...
...AND GIRLS.
IN MY EYES, EVERYONE WAS EQUALLY CAPABLE OF HARMING ME. SO WHY NOT?
I HAD BECOME EVERYTHING MY DAD CLAIMED HE HATED IN A PERSON, WITHOUT HIM KNOWING IT - A BEHAVIOUR SOME THOUGHT NEEDED CORRECTING.
Shane, this is Mrs. Caro.

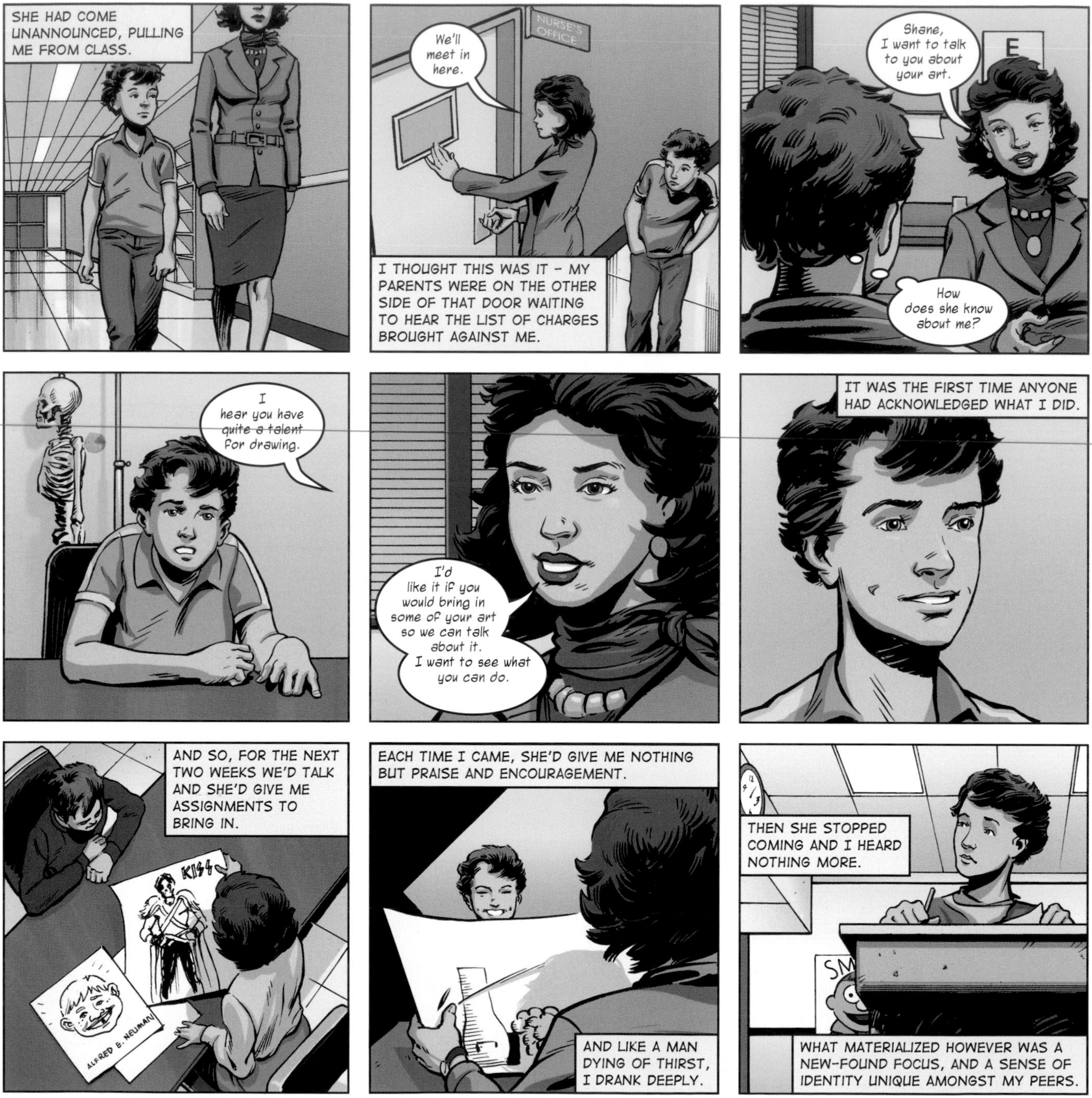
SHE HAD COME UNANNOUNCED, PULLING ME FROM CLASS.
NURSE'S OFFICE
We'll meet in here.
I THOUGHT THIS WAS IT – MY PARENTS WERE ON THE OTHER SIDE OF THAT DOOR WAITING TO HEAR THE LIST OF CHARGES BROUGHT AGAINST ME.
Shane, I want to talk to you about your art.
E
How does she know about me?
I hear you have quite a talent for drawing.
I'd like it if you would bring in some of your art so we can talk about it.
I want to see what you can do.
IT WAS THE FIRST TIME ANYONE HAD ACKNOWLEDGED WHAT I DID.
AND SO, FOR THE NEXT TWO WEEKS WE'D TALK AND SHE'D GIVE ME ASSIGNMENTS TO BRING IN.
KISS
ALFRED E. NEUMAN
EACH TIME I CAME, SHE'D GIVE ME NOTHING BUT PRAISE AND ENCOURAGEMENT.
AND LIKE A MAN DYING OF THIRST, I DRANK DEEPLY.
THEN SHE STOPPED COMING AND I HEARD NOTHING MORE.
WHAT MATERIALIZED HOWEVER WAS A NEW-FOUND FOCUS, AND A SENSE OF IDENTITY UNIQUE AMONGST MY PEERS.

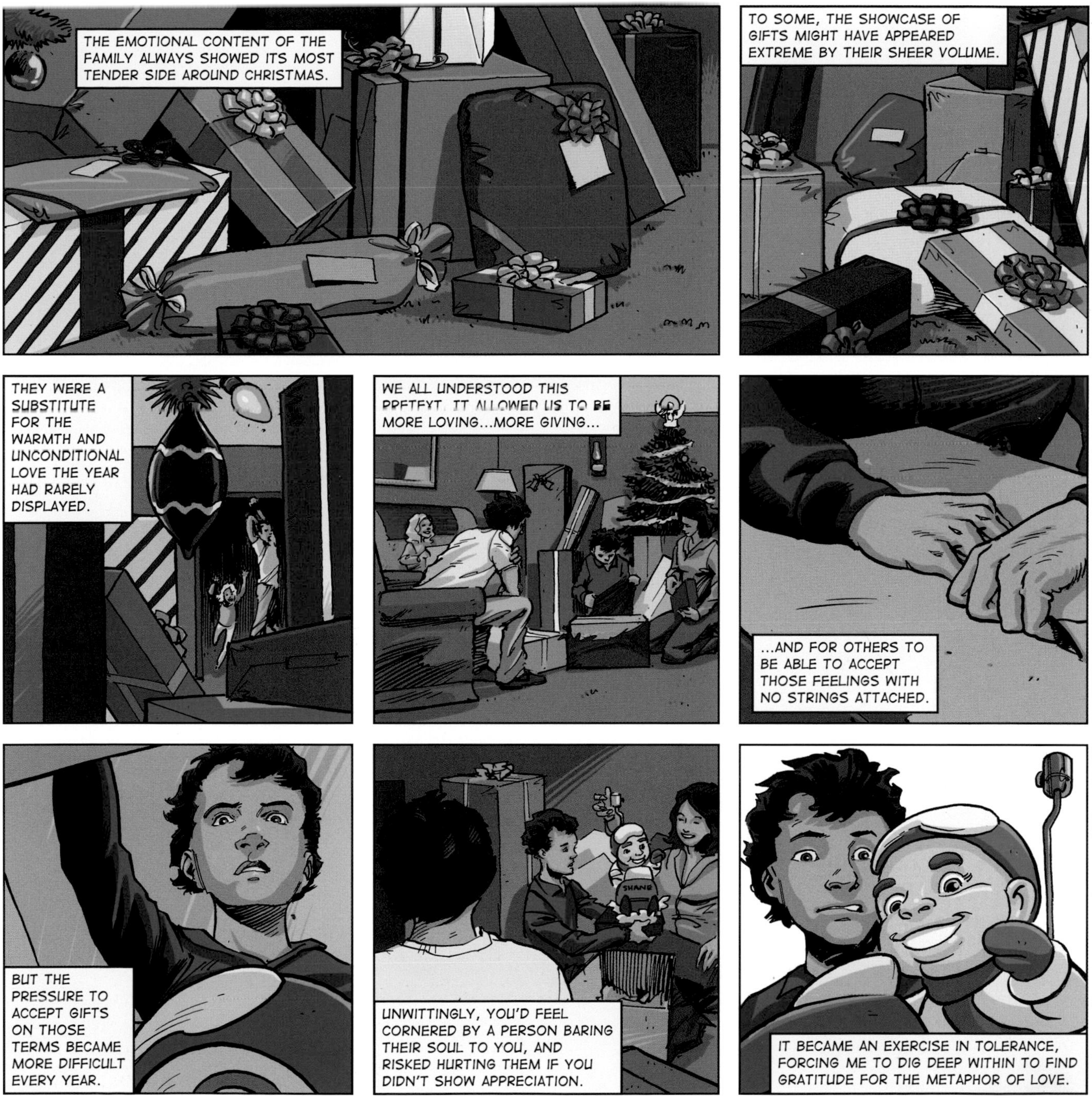
THE EMOTIONAL CONTENT OF THE FAMILY ALWAYS SHOWED ITS MOST TENDER SIDE AROUND CHRISTMAS.
TO SOME, THE SHOWCASE OF GIFTS MIGHT HAVE APPEARED EXTREME BY THEIR SHEER VOLUME.
THEY WERE A SUBSTITUTE FOR THE WARMTH AND UNCONDITIONAL LOVE THE YEAR HAD RARELY DISPLAYED.
WE ALL UNDERSTOOD THIS PRETEXT. IT ALLOWED US TO BE MORE LOVING...MORE GIVING...
...AND FOR OTHERS TO BE ABLE TO ACCEPT THOSE FEELINGS WITH NO STRINGS ATTACHED.
BUT THE PRESSURE TO ACCEPT GIFTS ON THOSE TERMS BECAME MORE DIFFICULT EVERY YEAR.
SHANE
UNWITTINGLY, YOU'D FEEL CORNERED BY A PERSON BARING THEIR SOUL TO YOU, AND RISKED HURTING THEM IF YOU DIDN'T SHOW APPRECIATION.
IT BECAME AN EXERCISE IN TOLERANCE, FORCING ME TO DIG DEEP WITHIN TO FIND GRATITUDE FOR THE METAPHOR OF LOVE.

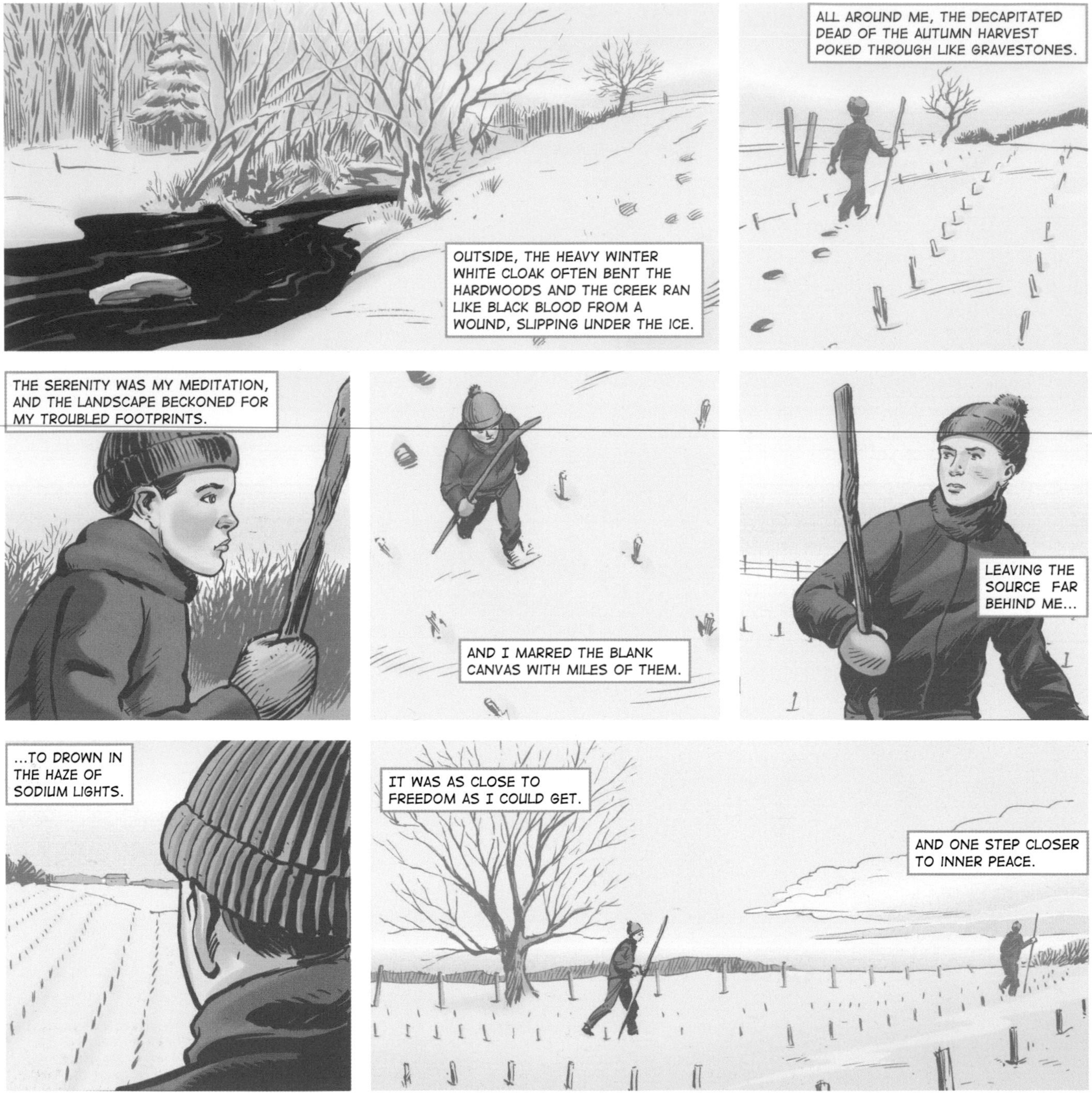
OUTSIDE, THE HEAVY WINTER WHITE CLOAK OFTEN BENT THE HARDWOODS AND THE CREEK RAN LIKE BLACK BLOOD FROM A WOUND, SLIPPING UNDER THE ICE.
ALL AROUND ME, THE DECAPITATED DEAD OF THE AUTUMN HARVEST POKED THROUGH LIKE GRAVESTONES.
THE SERENITY WAS MY MEDITATION, AND THE LANDSCAPE BECKONED FOR MY TROUBLED FOOTPRINTS.
AND I MARRED THE BLANK CANVAS WITH MILES OF THEM.
LEAVING THE SOURCE FAR BEHIND ME...
...TO DROWN IN THE HAZE OF SODIUM LIGHTS.
IT WAS AS CLOSE TO FREEDOM AS I COULD GET.
AND ONE STEP CLOSER TO INNER PEACE.

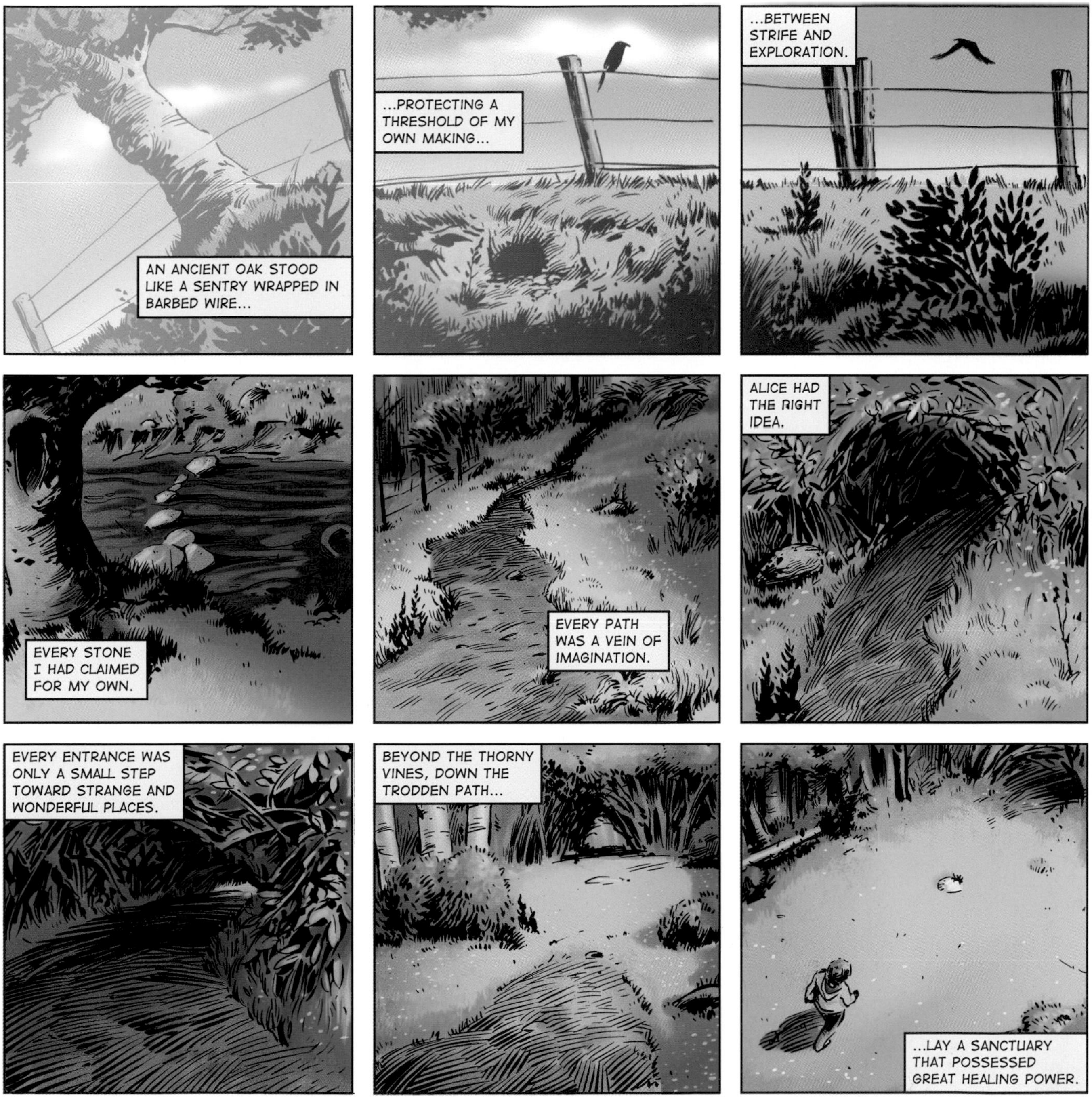
AN ANCIENT OAK STOOD LIKE A SENTRY WRAPPED IN BARBED WIRE...
...PROTECTING A THRESHOLD OF MY OWN MAKING...
...BETWEEN STRIFE AND EXPLORATION.
EVERY STONE I HAD CLAIMED FOR MY OWN.
EVERY PATH WAS A VEIN OF IMAGINATION.
ALICE HAD THE RIGHT IDEA.
EVERY ENTRANCE WAS ONLY A SMALL STEP TOWARD STRANGE AND WONDERFUL PLACES.
BEYOND THE THORNY VINES, DOWN THE TRODDEN PATH...
...LAY A SANCTUARY THAT POSSESSED GREAT HEALING POWER.

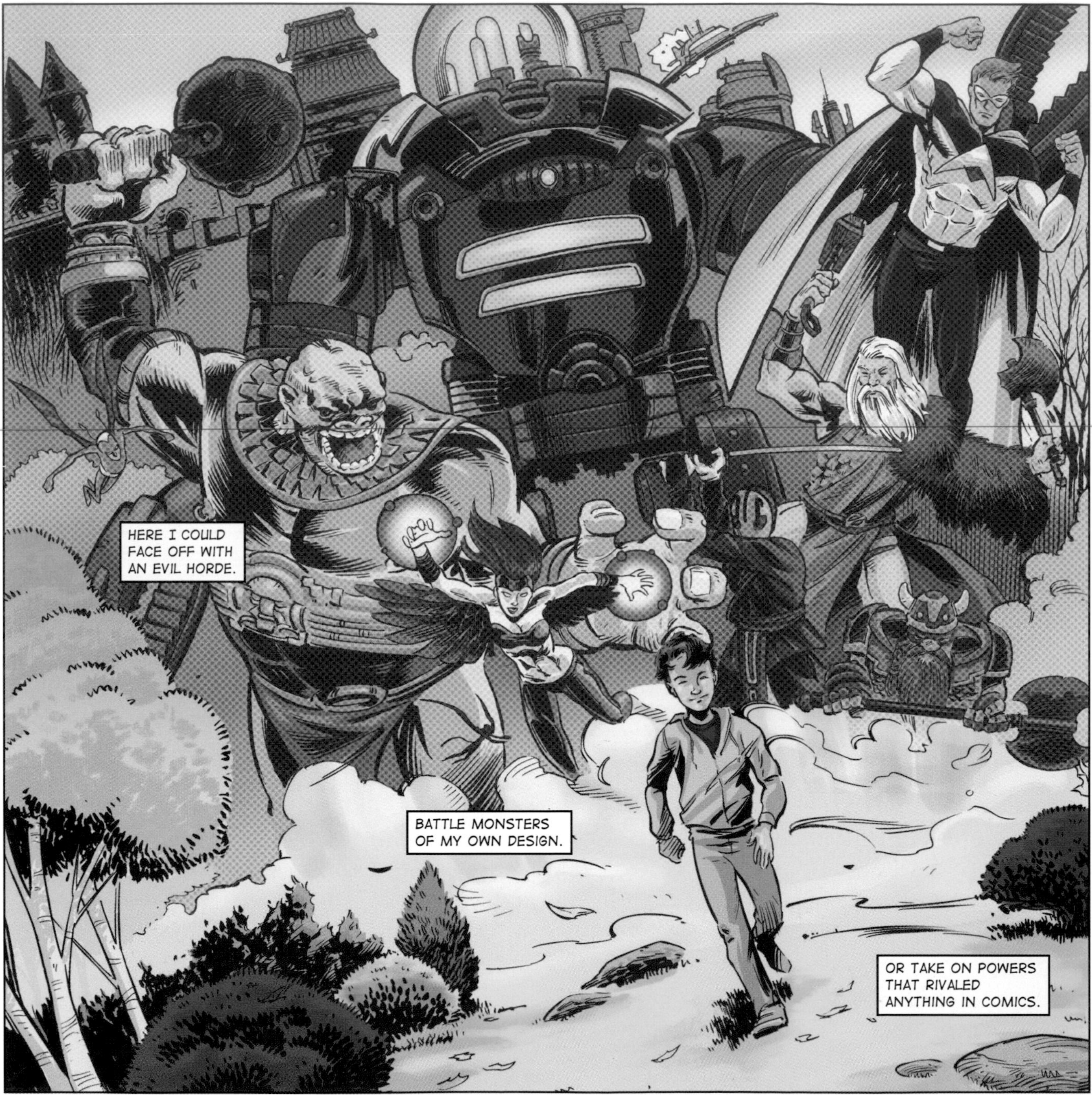
HERE I COULD FACE OFF WITH AN EVIL HORDE.
BATTLE MONSTERS OF MY OWN DESIGN.
OR TAKE ON POWERS THAT RIVALED ANYTHING IN COMICS.

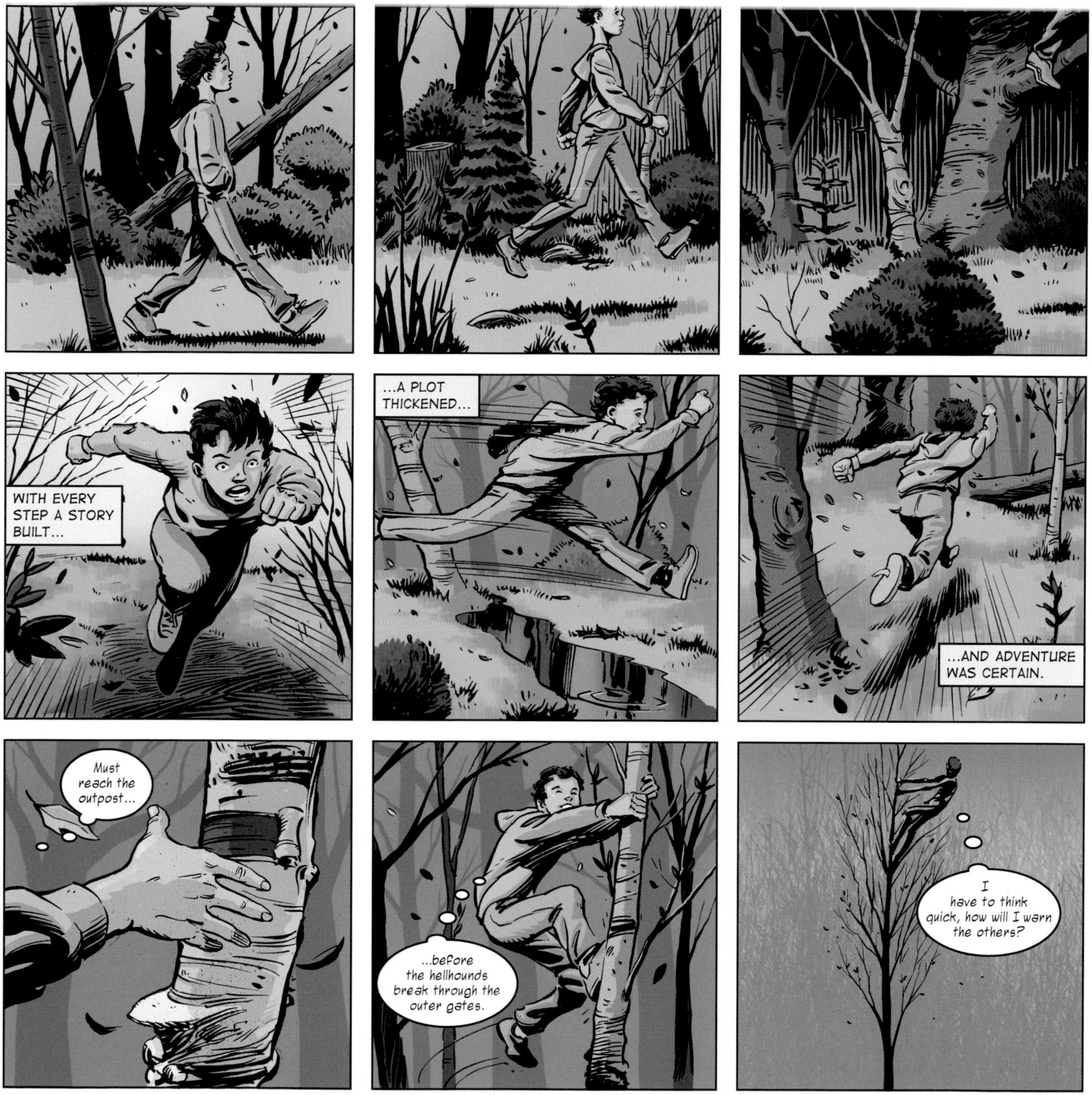
WITH EVERY STEP A STORY BUILT...
...A PLOT THICKENED...
...AND ADVENTURE WAS CERTAIN.
Must reach the outpost...
...before the hellhounds break through the outer gates.
I have to think quick, how will I warn the others?

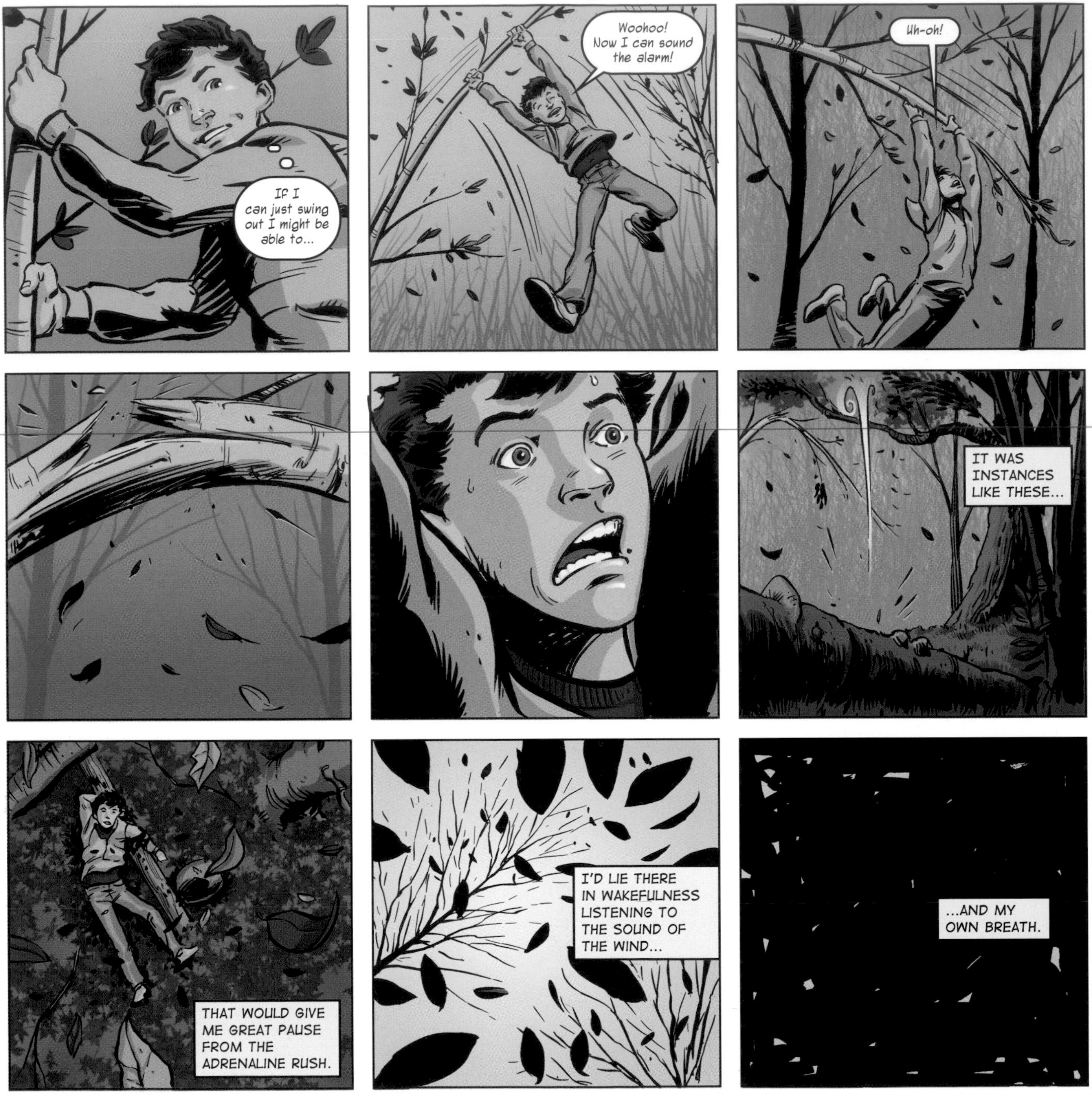
If I can just swing out I might be able to...
Woohoo! Now I can sound the alarm!
Uh-oh!
IT WAS INSTANCES LIKE THESE...
THAT WOULD GIVE ME GREAT PAUSE FROM THE ADRENALINE RUSH.
I'D LIE THERE IN WAKEFULNESS LISTENING TO THE SOUND OF THE WIND...
...AND MY OWN BREATH.

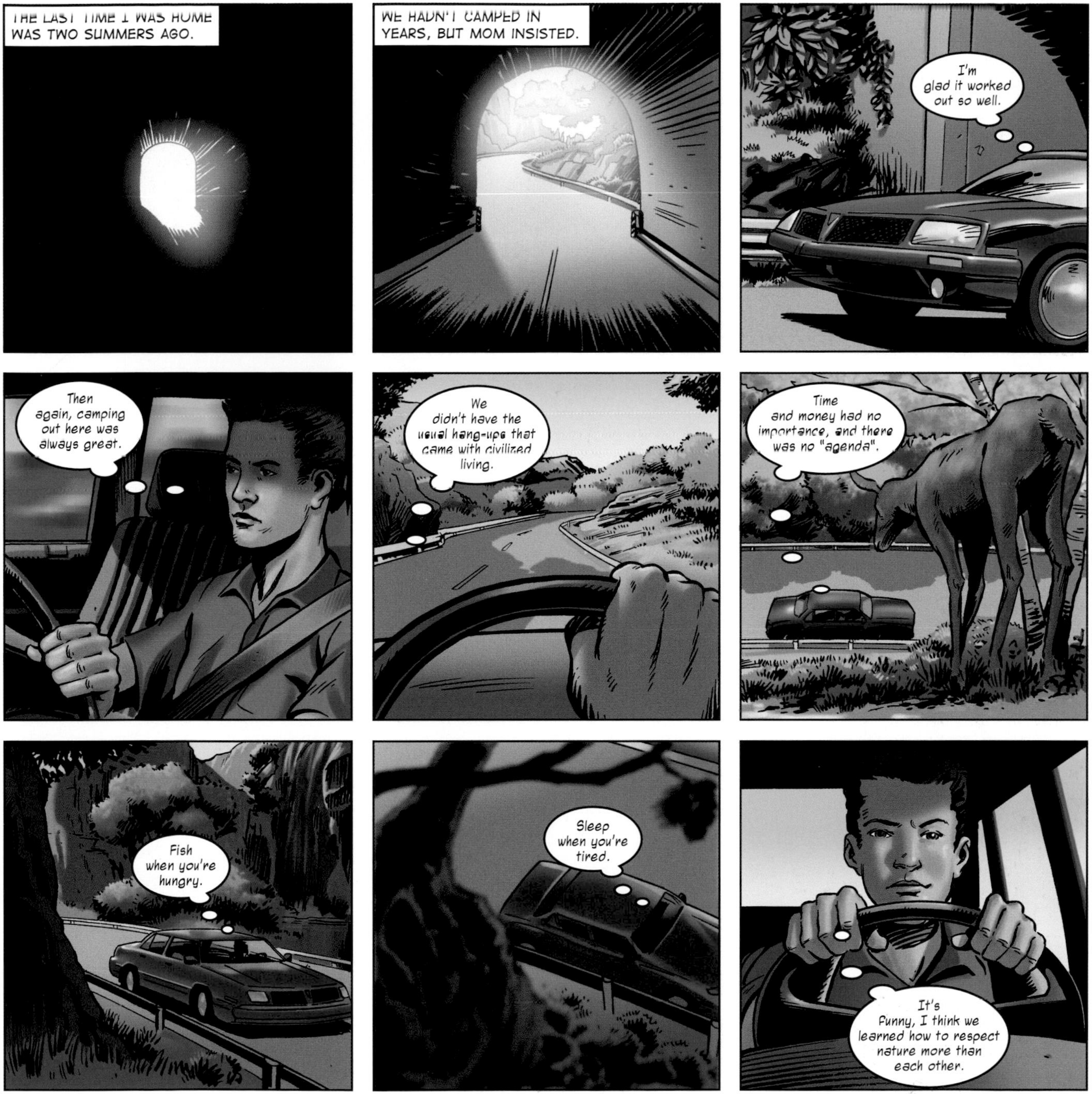
THE LAST TIME I WAS HOME WAS TWO SUMMERS AGO.
WE HADN'T CAMPED IN YEARS, BUT MOM INSISTED.
I'm glad it worked out so well.
Then again, camping out here was always great.
We didn't have the usual hang-ups that came with civilized living.
Time and money had no importance, and there was no "agenda".
Fish when you're hungry.
Sleep when you're tired.
It's funny, I think we learned how to respect nature more than each other.

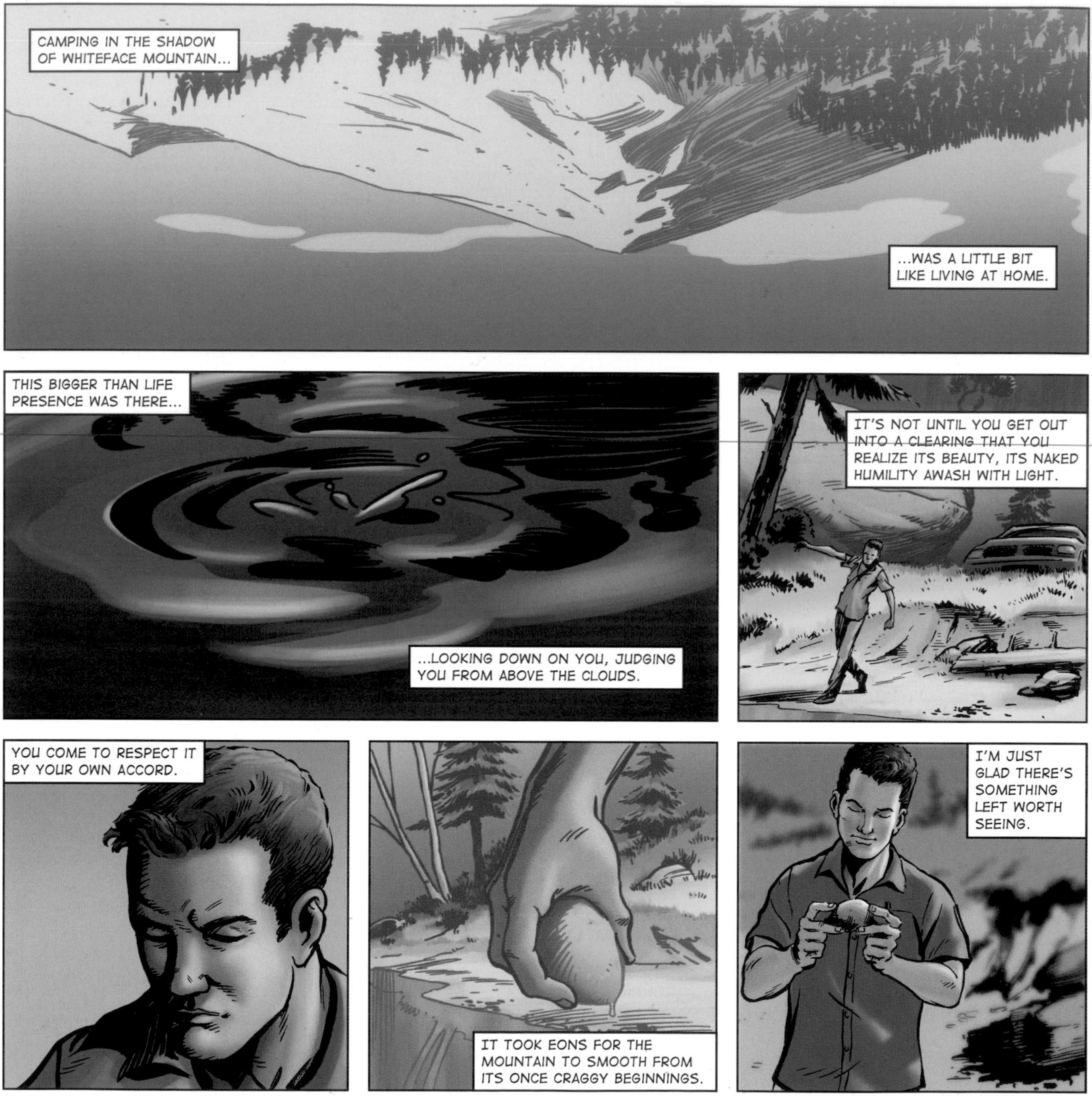
CAMPING IN THE SHADOW OF WHITEFACE MOUNTAIN...
...WAS A LITTLE BIT LIKE LIVING AT HOME.
THIS BIGGER THAN LIFE PRESENCE WAS THERE...
...LOOKING DOWN ON YOU, JUDGING YOU FROM ABOVE THE CLOUDS.
IT'S NOT UNTIL YOU GET OUT INTO A CLEARING THAT YOU REALIZE ITS BEAUTY, ITS NAKED HUMILITY AWASH WITH LIGHT.
YOU COME TO RESPECT IT BY YOUR OWN ACCORD.
IT TOOK EONS FOR THE MOUNTAIN TO SMOOTH FROM ITS ONCE CRAGGY BEGINNINGS.
I'M JUST GLAD THERE'S SOMETHING LEFT WORTH SEEING.

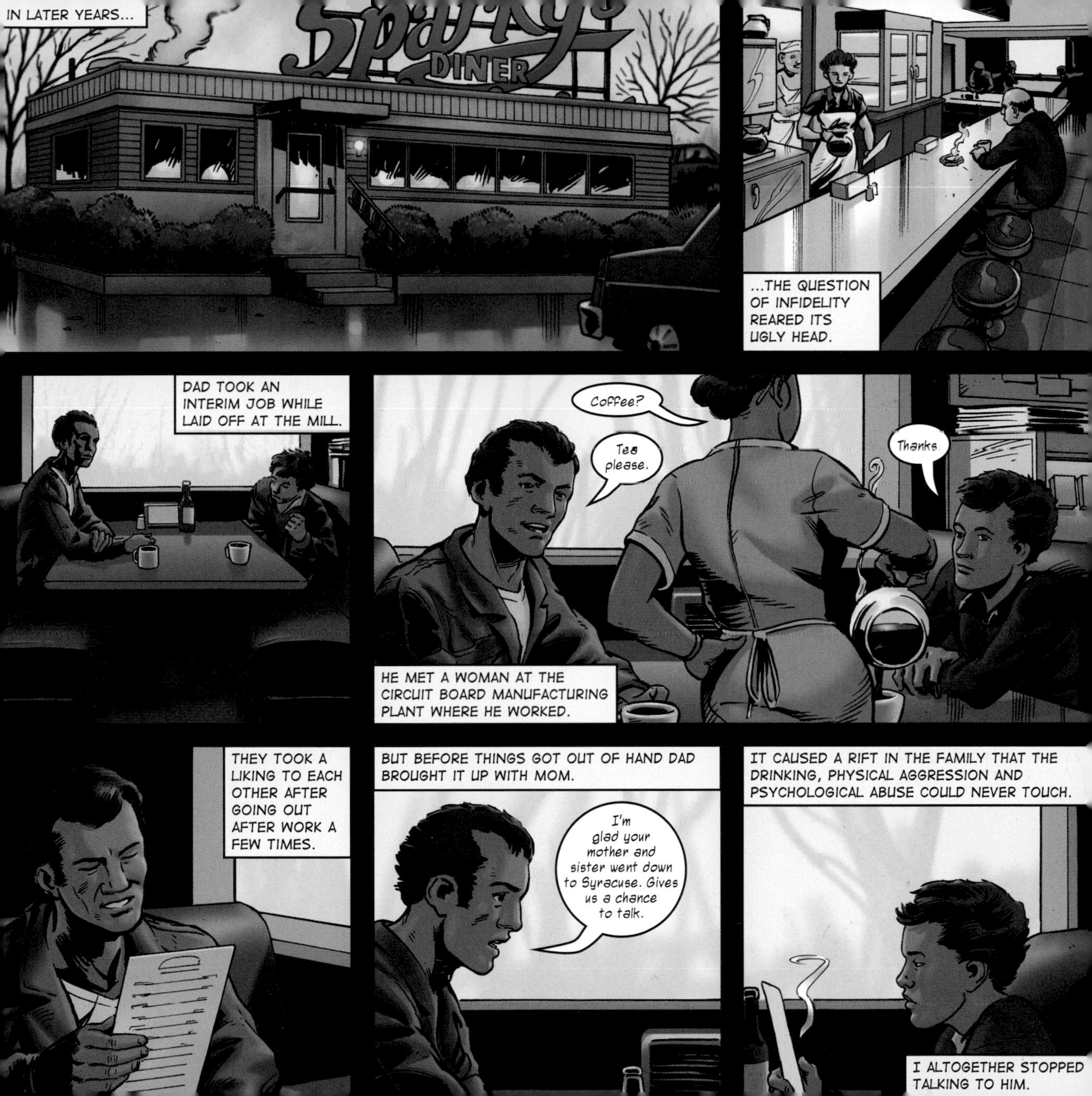
IN LATER YEARS...
Sparky's DINER
...THE QUESTION OF INFIDELITY REARED ITS UGLY HEAD.
DAD TOOK AN INTERIM JOB WHILE LAID OFF AT THE MILL.
Coffee?
Tea please.
Thanks.
HE MET A WOMAN AT THE CIRCUIT BOARD MANUFACTURING PLANT WHERE HE WORKED.
THEY TOOK A LIKING TO EACH OTHER AFTER GOING OUT AFTER WORK A FEW TIMES.
BUT BEFORE THINGS GOT OUT OF HAND DAD BROUGHT IT UP WITH MOM.
I'm glad your mother and sister went down to Syracuse. Gives us a chance to talk.
IT CAUSED A RIFT IN THE FAMILY THAT THE DRINKING, PHYSICAL AGGRESSION AND PSYCHOLOGICAL ABUSE COULD NEVER TOUCH.
I ALTOGETHER STOPPED TALKING TO HIM.

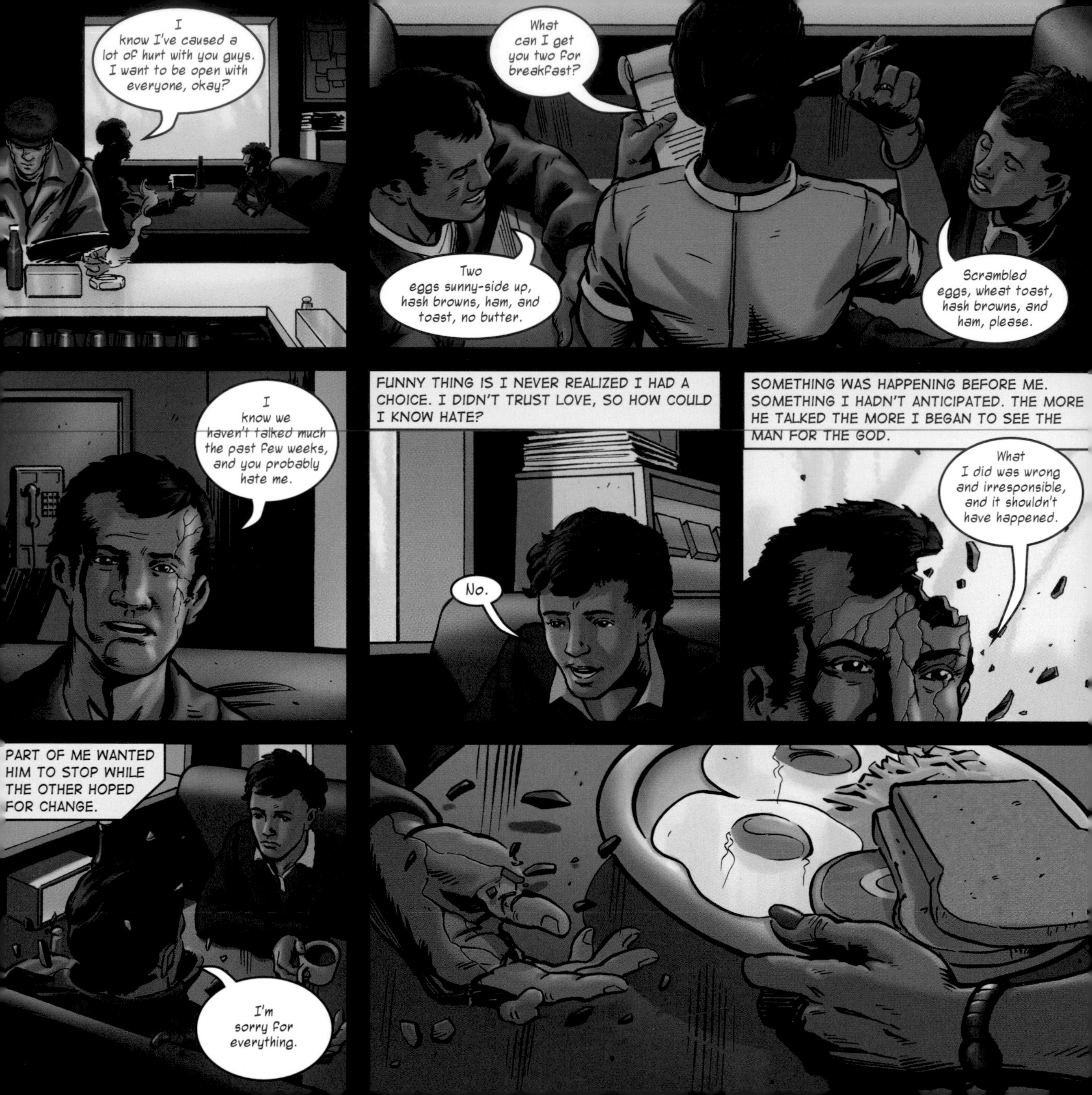
I know I've caused a lot of hurt with you guys. I want to be open with everyone, okay?
What can I get you two for breakfast?
Two eggs sunny-side up, hash browns, ham, and toast, no butter.
Scrambled eggs, wheat toast, hash browns, and ham, please.
I know we haven't talked much the past few weeks, and you probably hate me.
FUNNY THING IS I NEVER REALIZED I HAD A CHOICE. I DIDN'T TRUST LOVE, SO HOW COULD I KNOW HATE?
No.
SOMETHING WAS HAPPENING BEFORE ME. SOMETHING I HADN'T ANTICIPATED. THE MORE HE TALKED THE MORE I BEGAN TO SEE THE MAN FOR THE GOD.
What I did was wrong and irresponsible, and it shouldn't have happened.
PART OF ME WANTED HIM TO STOP WHILE THE OTHER HOPED FOR CHANGE.
I'm sorry for everything.

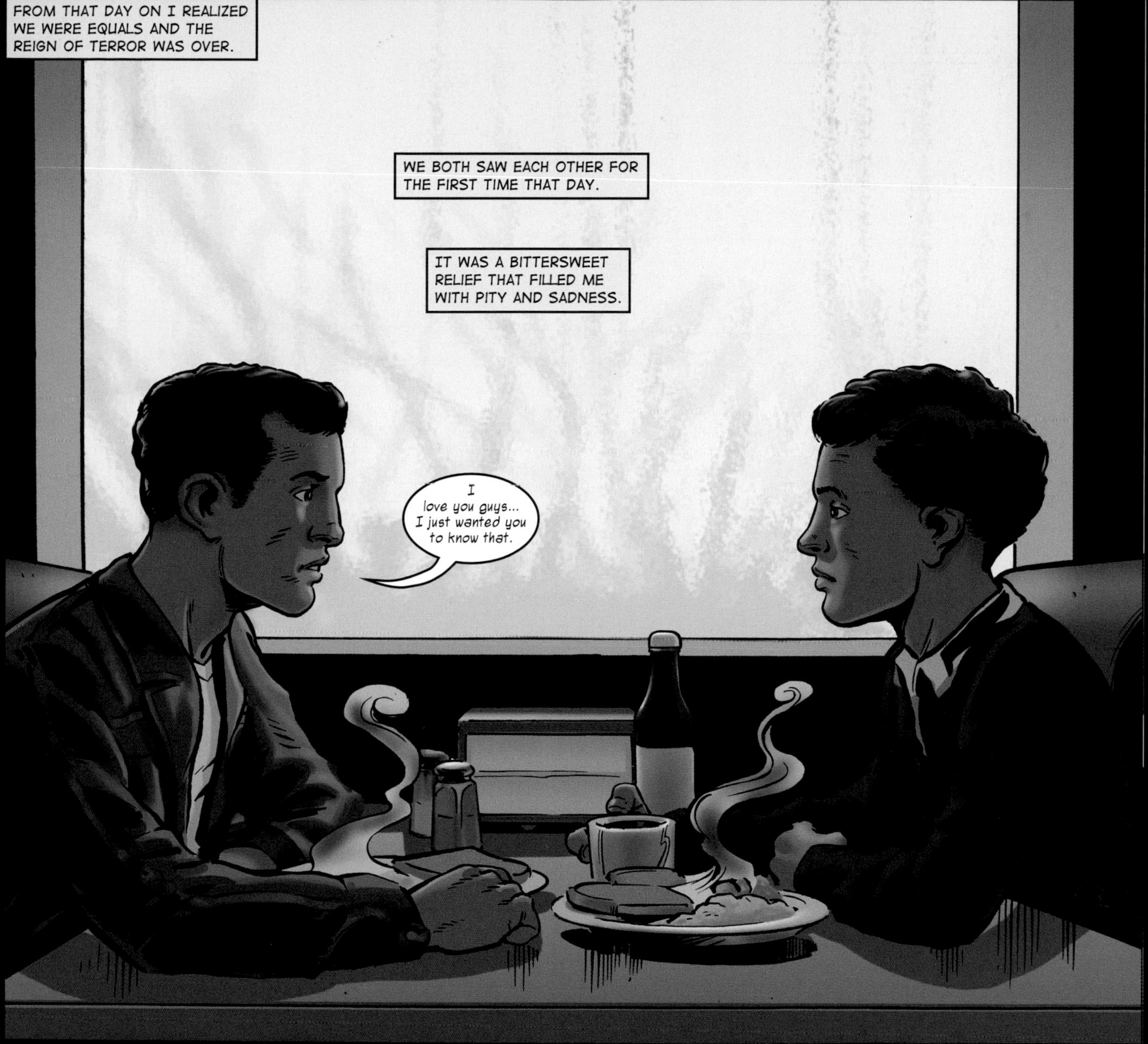
FROM THAT DAY ON I REALIZED WE WERE EQUALS AND THE REIGN OF TERROR WAS OVER.
WE BOTH SAW EACH OTHER FOR THE FIRST TIME THAT DAY.
IT WAS A BITTERSWEET RELIEF THAT FILLED ME WITH PITY AND SADNESS.
I love you guys... I just wanted you to know that.

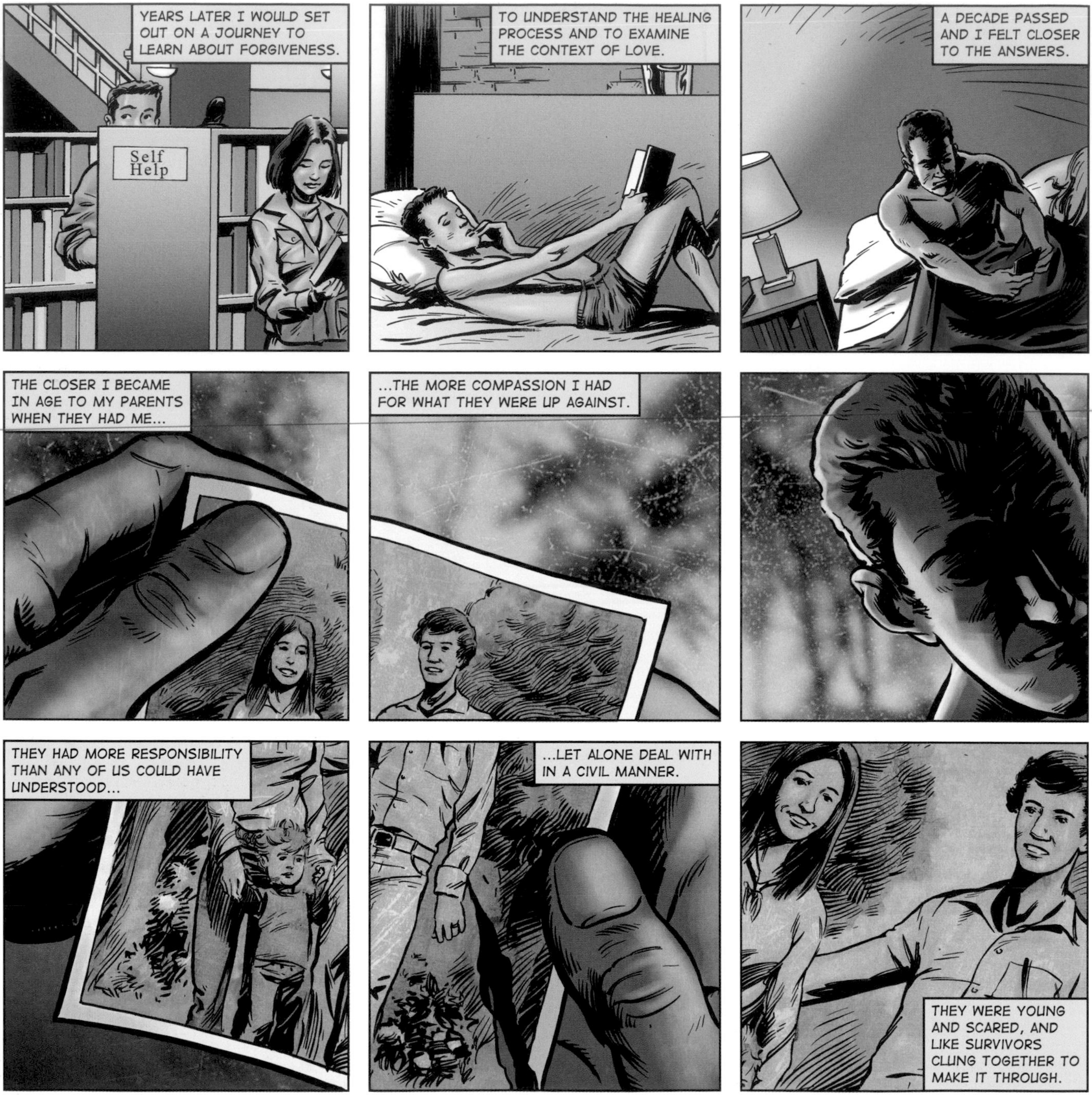
YEARS LATER I WOULD SET OUT ON A JOURNEY TO LEARN ABOUT FORGIVENESS.
Self Help
TO UNDERSTAND THE HEALING PROCESS AND TO EXAMINE THE CONTEXT OF LOVE.
A DECADE PASSED AND I FELT CLOSER TO THE ANSWERS.
THE CLOSER I BECAME IN AGE TO MY PARENTS WHEN THEY HAD ME...
...THE MORE COMPASSION I HAD FOR WHAT THEY WERE UP AGAINST.
THEY HAD MORE RESPONSIBILITY THAN ANY OF US COULD HAVE UNDERSTOOD...
...LET ALONE DEAL WITH IN A CIVIL MANNER.
THEY WERE YOUNG AND SCARED, AND LIKE SURVIVORS CLUNG TOGETHER TO MAKE IT THROUGH.

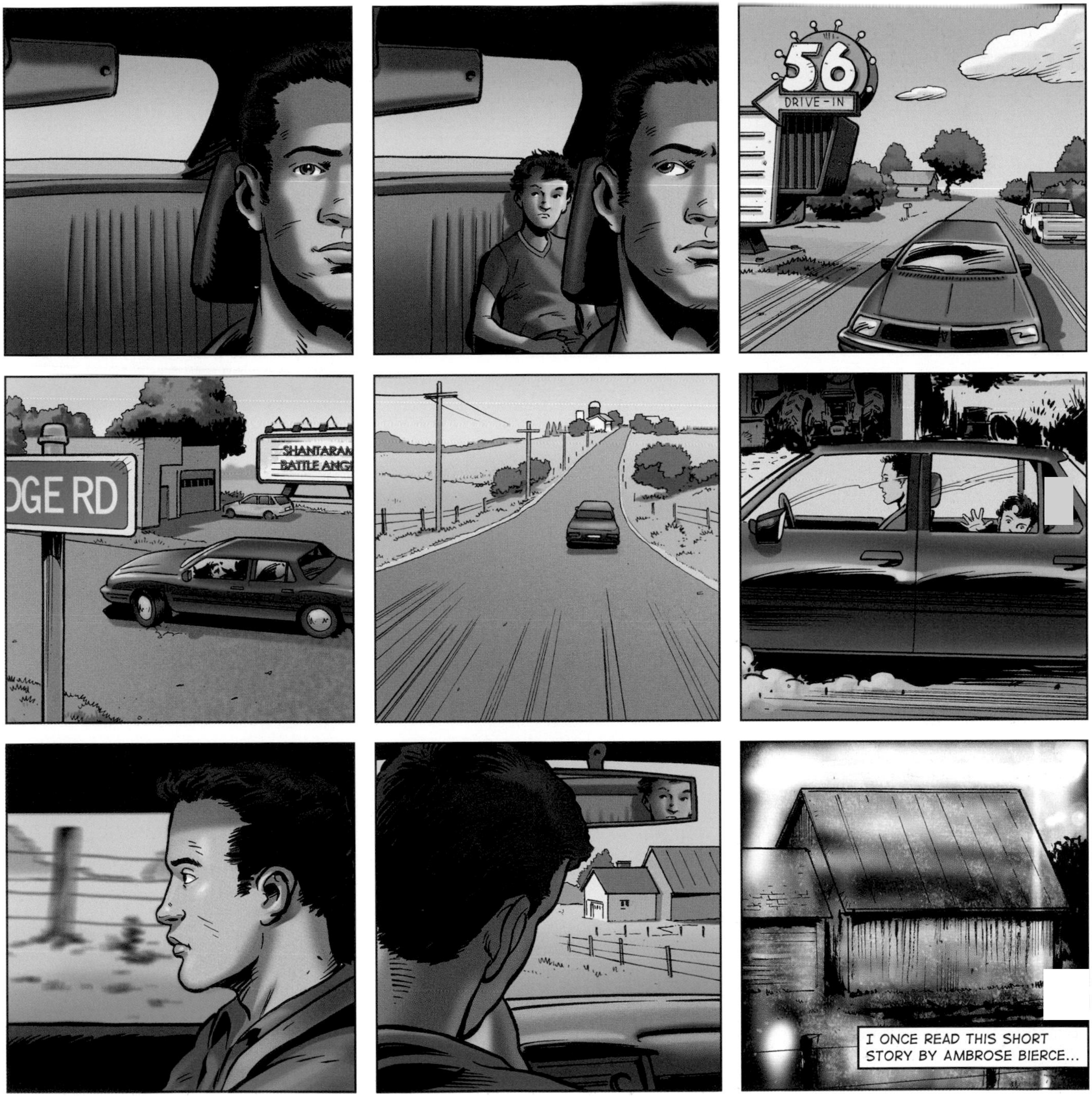
56
DRIVE-IN
DGE RD
SHANTARAM
BATTLE ANG
I ONCE READ THIS SHORT STORY BY AMBROSE BIERCE...

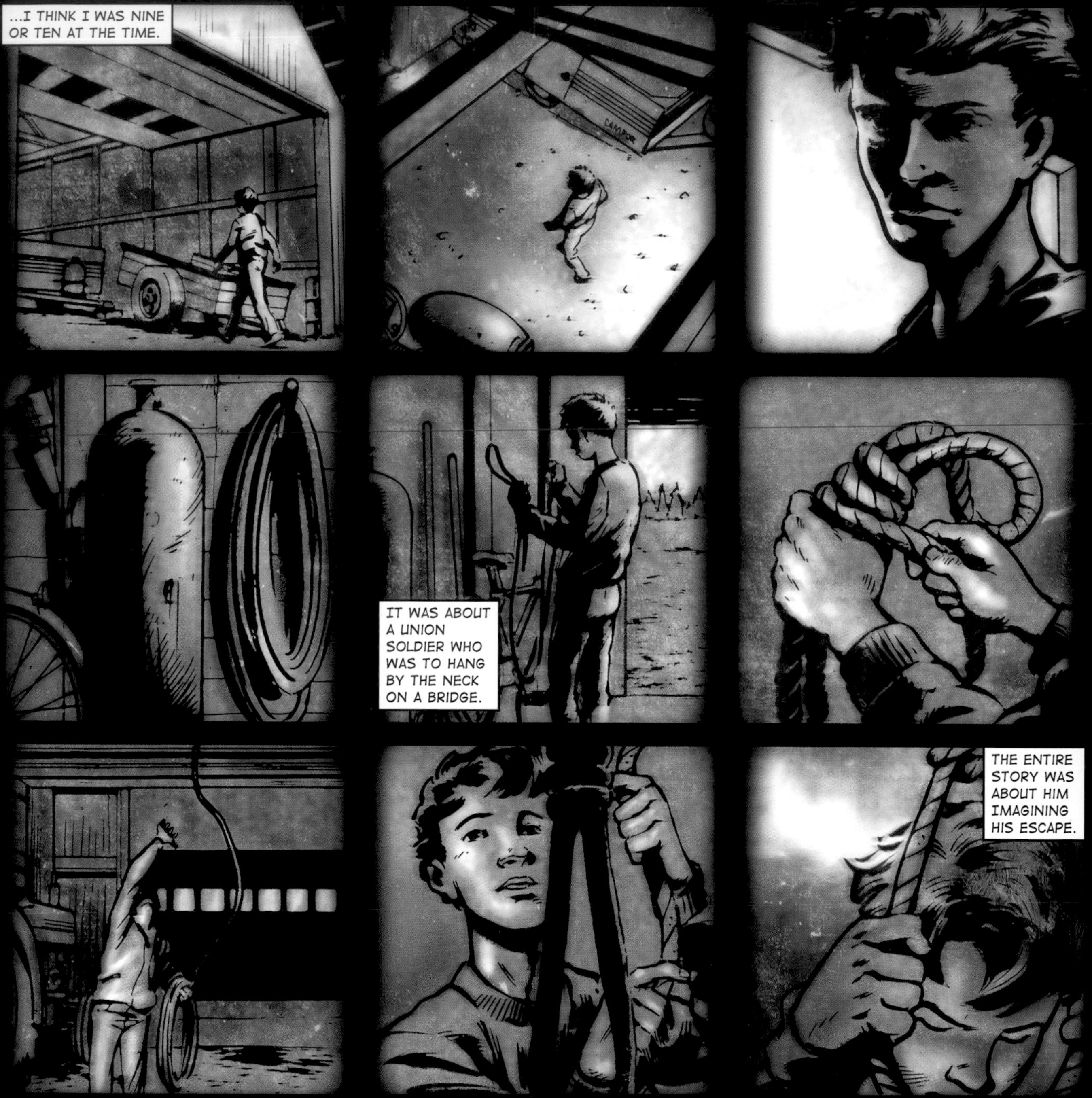
...I THINK I WAS NINE OR TEN AT THE TIME.
IT WAS ABOUT A UNION SOLDIER WHO WAS TO HANG BY THE NECK ON A BRIDGE.
THE ENTIRE STORY WAS ABOUT HIM IMAGINING HIS ESCAPE.

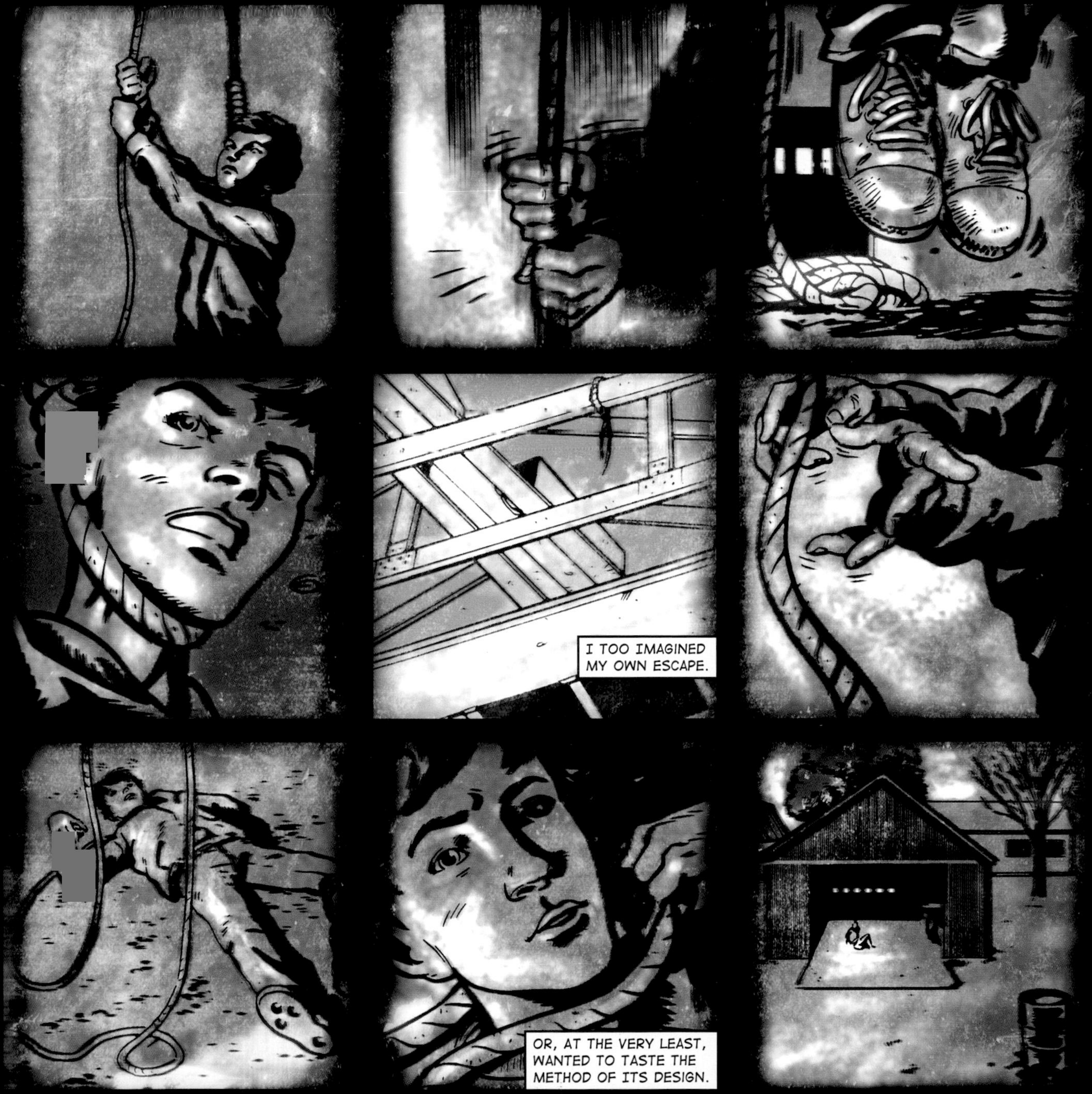
I TOO IMAGINED MY OWN ESCAPE.
OR, AT THE VERY LEAST, WANTED TO TASTE THE METHOD OF ITS DESIGN.

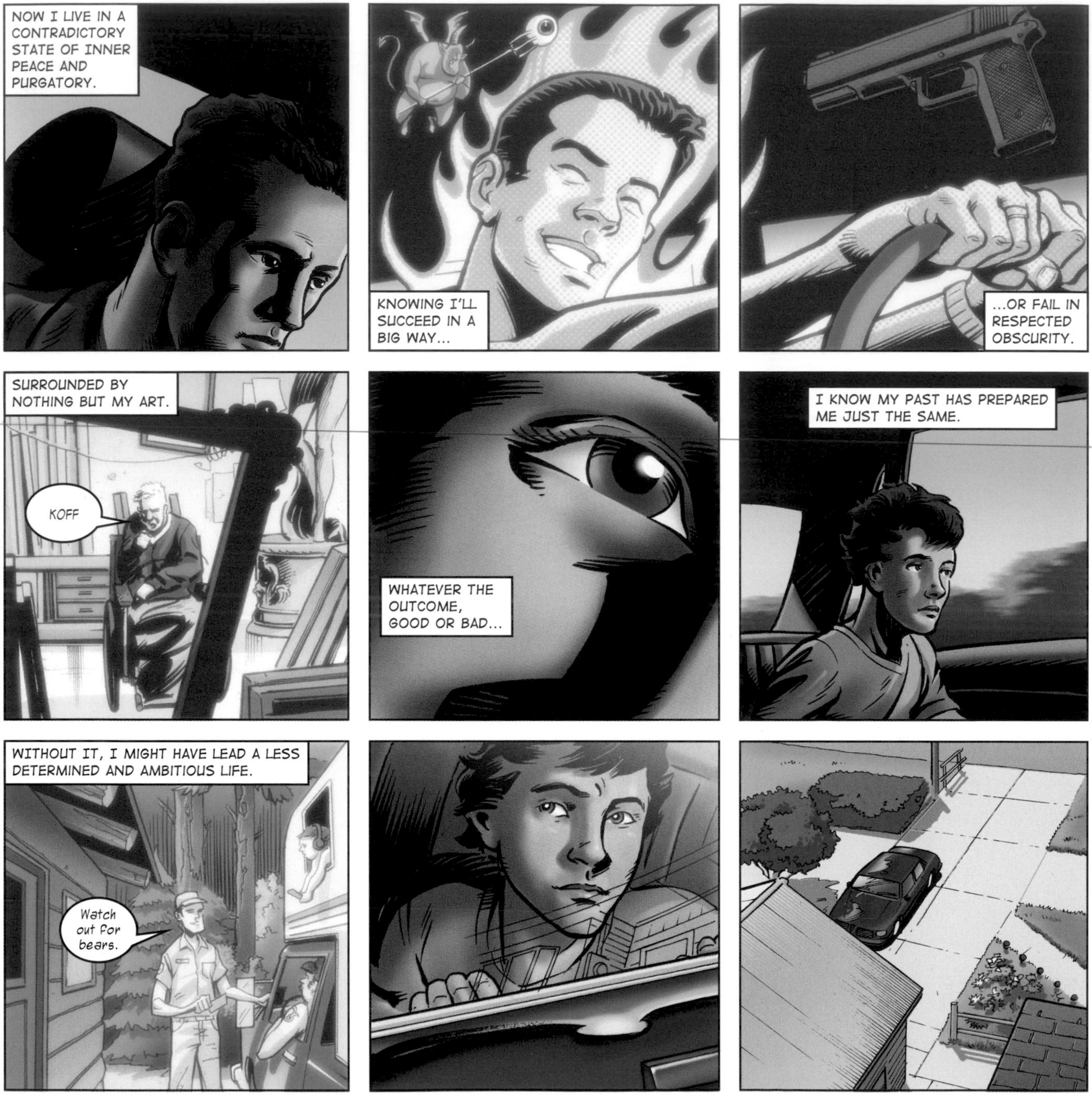
NOW I LIVE IN A CONTRADICTORY STATE OF INNER PEACE AND PURGATORY.
KNOWING I'LL SUCCEED IN A BIG WAY...
...OR FAIL IN RESPECTED OBSCURITY.
SURROUNDED BY NOTHING BUT MY ART.
KOFF
WHATEVER THE OUTCOME, GOOD OR BAD...
I KNOW MY PAST HAS PREPARED ME JUST THE SAME.
WITHOUT IT, I MIGHT HAVE LEAD A LESS DETERMINED AND AMBITIOUS LIFE.
Watch out for bears.

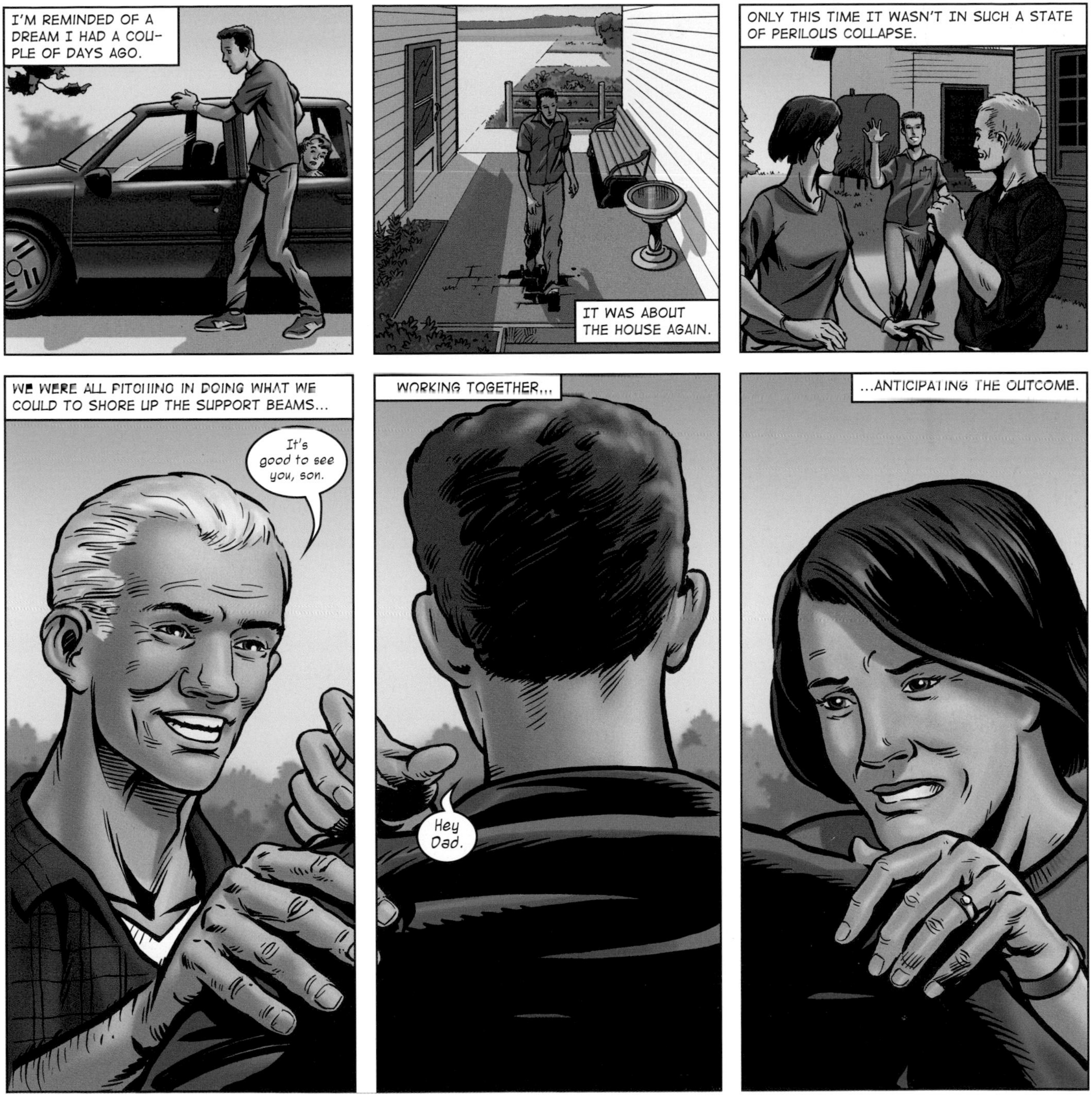
I'M REMINDED OF A DREAM I HAD A COUPLE OF DAYS AGO.
IT WAS ABOUT THE HOUSE AGAIN.
ONLY THIS TIME IT WASN'T IN SUCH A STATE OF PERILOUS COLLAPSE.
WE WERE ALL PITCHING IN DOING WHAT WE COULD TO SHORE UP THE SUPPORT BEAMS...
It's good to see you, son.
WORKING TOGETHER...
Hey Dad.
...ANTICIPATING THE OUTCOME.

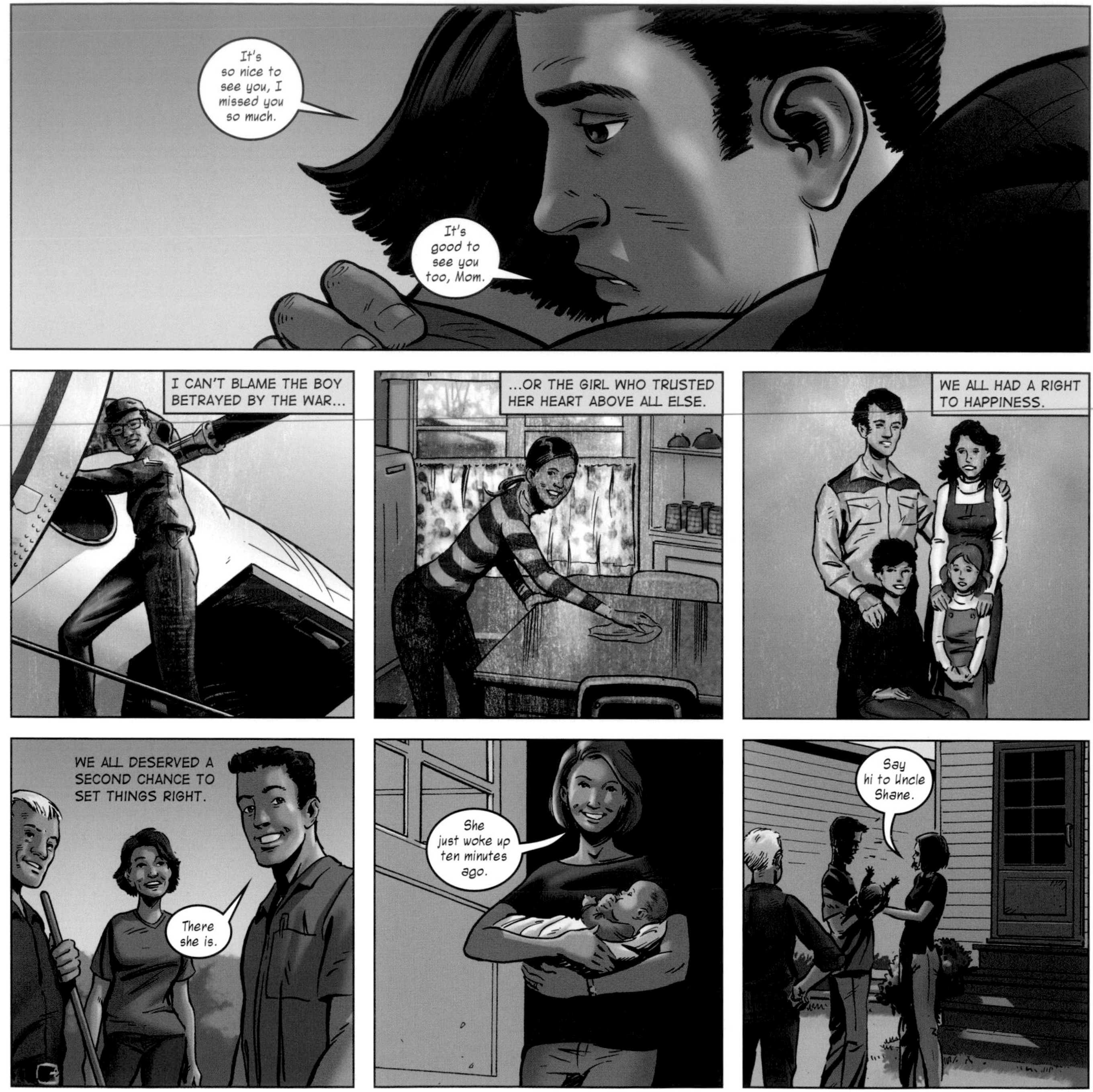

It's so nice to see you, I missed you so much.
It's good to see you too, Mom.
I CAN'T BLAME THE BOY BETRAYED BY THE WAR...
...OR THE GIRL WHO TRUSTED HER HEART ABOVE ALL ELSE.
WE ALL HAD A RIGHT TO HAPPINESS.
WE ALL DESERVED A SECOND CHANCE TO SET THINGS RIGHT.
There she is.
She just woke up ten minutes ago.
Say hi to Uncle Shane.

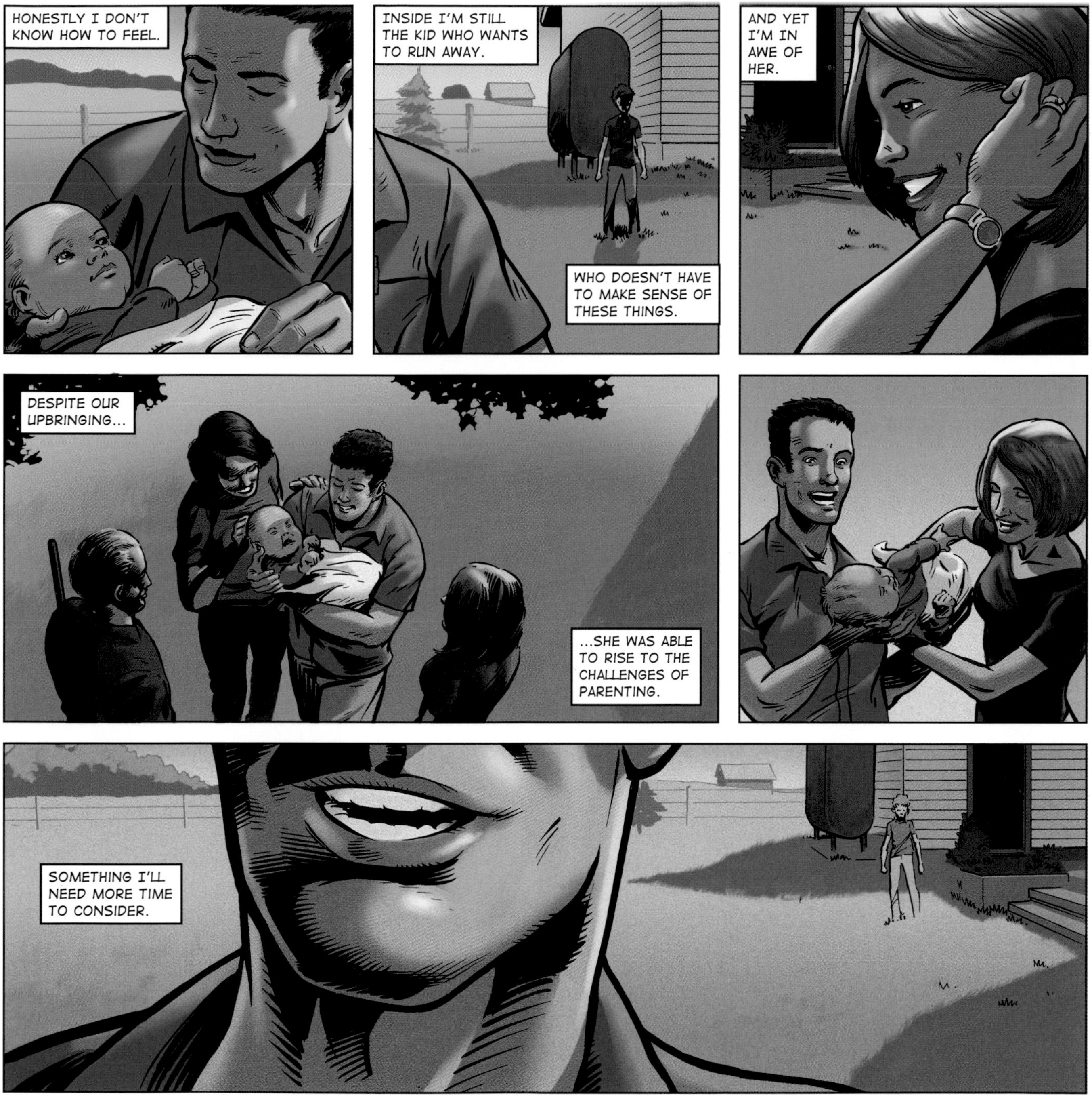
HONESTLY I DON'T KNOW HOW TO FEEL.
INSIDE I'M STILL THE KID WHO WANTS TO RUN AWAY.
WHO DOESN'T HAVE TO MAKE SENSE OF THESE THINGS.
AND YET I'M IN AWE OF HER.
DESPITE OUR UPBRINGING...
...SHE WAS ABLE TO RISE TO THE CHALLENGES OF PARENTING.
SOMETHING I'LL NEED MORE TIME TO CONSIDER.

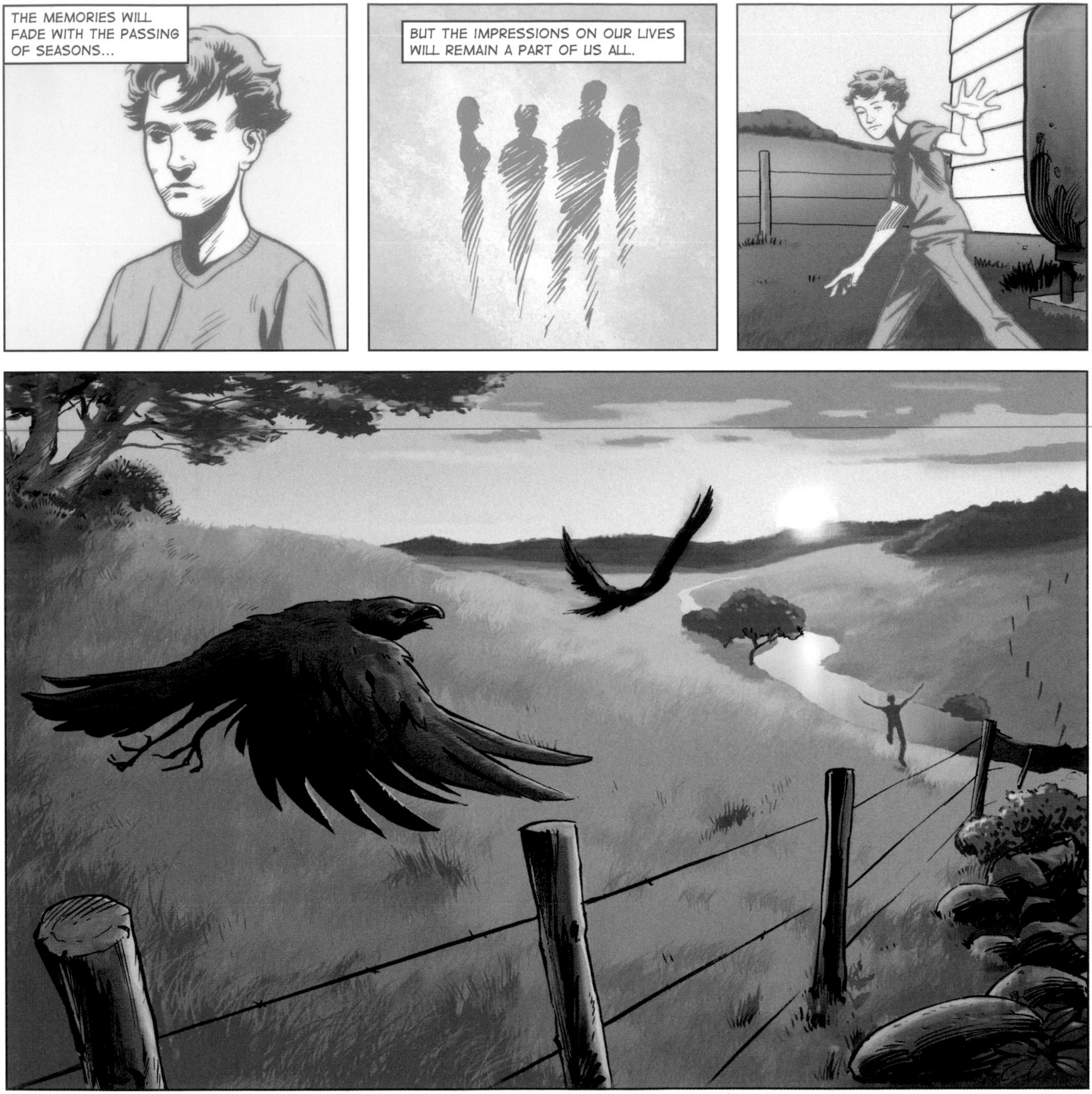
THE MEMORIES WILL FADE WITH THE PASSING OF SEASONS...
BUT THE IMPRESSIONS ON OUR LIVES WILL REMAIN A PART OF US ALL.

The author circa 1970

To Mom, Dad and Terra

Recently from ComicsLit:
Ordinary Victories, full color, 120pp., $15.95
Lucifer's Garden of Verses:
to be in 4 volumes. Each 80pp., b&w, cloth: $15.95, pb.: $8.95.
(S3 P&H 1st item, $1 each addt'l)

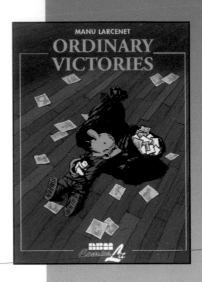

We have over 200 graphic novels in stock, ask for our color catalog:
NBM
555 8th Ave., Suite 1202
New York, NY 10018
www.nbmpublishing.com